SECRET UNDERGROUND
LONDON

SECRET UNDERGROUND
LONDON

Nick Catford

FOLLY BOOKS

Published by Folly Books Ltd
Monkton Farleigh
BA15 2QP
www.follybooks.co.uk

Designed and typeset by Vicky

Printed and bound in India by Replika Press Pvt Ltd.

Jacket and introductory photographs:

Front jacket: Coffins in the catacomb at West Norwood cemetery.

Rear jacket: The abandoned low-level platform at Wood Lane station, closed 22 November 1947.

Facing title page: Accessed via a disused interchange subway at the far end of the northbound Bakerloo
Line platform at Embankment station, this huge chamber beneath Villiers Street once housed the
Embankment substation. For many years this supplied a large section of the underground railway
system with traction current. It was abandoned in 1957 when a new substation was opened near
Victoria Embankment Gardens. In October 2011 the Villiers Street site was brought back into use
and three new 2,500kW transformer-rectifiers installed.

CONTENTS

PREFACE

This book is the culmination of a fifty-year fascination with the industrial archaeology of the British Isles as a whole and of London and southeast England in particular. Initially, I wanted to make a photographic record of the network of derelict canals and waterways that, by the early 1960s, were fast passing into oblivion, and of the many railway lines that, as a consequence of the Beeching cuts, were following in their wake. At the same time, Britain's old and obsolete industrial base was in decline and many of the old mills, factories and warehouses, often dating from the Victorian era, lay disused, derelict and awaiting demolition. This fascination with the visible relics of bygone industry that littered Britain's landscape had, by 1980, extended to encompass the country's abandoned, man-made subterranean infrastructure, from mines and quarries to abandoned tube lines and stations. From there it was just a short step to a study of the secret underground world, now largely lying derelict, created during the Second World War and, later, in response to the threats that faced the nation throughout the Cold War years.

From the outset, I realised that to tell the whole story of London's secret underworld and explain the way in which the various elements developed and interacted, it would be necessary to extend beyond the confines of the inner city. I have included, for example, reference to the Surrey stone quarries, which were not only an important source of building material for the City up until the eighteenth century, but also provided safe sanctuary for artefacts from London's museums during the Second World War. For this book, then, I have defined London as the area lying within the M25 motorway and, even allowing for this broad definition, I have stepped across the border on more than one occasion where important underground structures have particular relevance. The Southern Railway wartime control centre at Deepdene House, and the once top-secret military communications centre, buried somewhat bizarrely beneath the car park at Wentworth Golf Club, are examples of this.

Most of the photographs that illustrate this book were taken by the author, but others have generously contributed images where gaps might otherwise have been left. For these I would like to thank the following:

Bourne Hall Museum: page 278; Alan Bradshaw: 189 (bottom left); J.E Connor: pages 29 (upper) and 35; Bob Jenner: page 153, 193 (top right); Roger Marks: page 214; John Palmer: 189 (bottom right), and Messrs Gilbey: page 219. The image of Blackheath Hill station on page 118 is from the Nick Catford collection and those on pages 145 (top right) and 155 (top left) are from the Subterranea Britannica collection.

I would also like to thank the following for providing the maps, plans and drawings that have helped, perhaps, to make this book more comprehensible:

J.E Connor: page 207
R.F LeGear and H. Pearman: pages 140 and 252
Roger Morgan: page 153
Tim Robinson: pages 14, 16, 46, 61, 62, 108, 148, 160, 245, 249.
Other plans were specially produced by Folly Books Ltd.

Particular thanks are offered to Peter Burgess and Paul Sowan for the quarry layout information included in the plans of the Surrey underground quarries reproduced on pages 257 and 269. Thanks are due also to Peter Darley, of the Camden Railway Heritage Trust, for his assistance regarding the history of the Camden railway vaults and horse tunnels.

Finally, I would like to extend my gratitude to the many members of Subterranea Brittanica who have contributed to the society's website (from which much information for this book has been drawn), and to my four proof-readers: Martin Dixon, Bob Jenner, Stewart Wild and Paul Sowan.

Nick Catford
December 2012

Chapter 1

INTRODUCTION

Over the last thirty years or so, hundreds of books have been written about London and its environs, and scores more have been written about the City's secretive and seedier corners. Alongside these there have appeared a handful of books dealing more or less exclusively with the less obvious, subterranean aspects of the city's social history. Predictably, two features of London's underground topography have dominated all these previous publications: London's lost rivers and Sir Joseph Bazalgette's Great Interceptor Sewers.

There is nothing left to say that has not already been said about the rivers that run beneath the streets of London, and they will get no further mention here. And, anyway, this is essentially a photographic record of underground London and the rivers are, for the most part, aesthetically unphotogenic and, practically, unphotographable. Sir Joseph and his sewers get a mention in chapter nineteen, but in connection with a less well known (although equally fascinating) aspect of Bazalgette's work, the Abbey Mills pumping station, rather than with the sewers themselves.

This is a book about industrial archaeology, supplemented by an investigation of those aspects of London's cultural and military history that have left permanent evidence of their passing in stone and concrete, brick and iron, beneath the city streets. All the underground structures illustrated in this book are man-made and all, with the exception of the Thames Barrier tunnels, are now disused and abandoned. With rising sea levels there is talk already of a new and bigger Thames barrier further to the east, so it seems likely that in the not so distant future the tunnels beneath the current barrier will be abandoned too.

Much of London's secret subterranean infrastructure, and by far the greater part of that described in this book, was both created and abandoned within the short temporal span of the twentieth century, and most, but not all, is directly associated with transport or with war. It is true that the first of London's underground railways was constructed in the nineteenth century; the first section of the Metropolitan Railway was opened in 1863 and the City & South London, the first true tube railway, as opposed to cut-and-cover tunnel,

in 1890, but these in many respects were just the early beginnings.

The real momentum in railway tunnelling through the London clay took hold in the first decade of the twentieth century under the commercial impetus of the entrepreneur Charles Tyson Yerkes, and the engineering genius of James Henry Greathead. Greathead was a contemporary of Peter Barlow who, in 1864, had patented a circular tunnelling shield. In 1869 the two men began work on the Tower Subway – only the second passage to be excavated under the Thames after Marc Brunel's disaster-ridden tunnel of 1843 – using a shield based upon Barlow's principles but much improved by Greathead and later attributed to him.

The Greathead shield was used to dig the tunnels for the City & South London Railway and was so successful that it went on to become, through various iterations, the means by which all the tube railways beneath London were subsequently excavated. Without Greathead's invention for boring the tunnels, and the millions of Cleveland cast-iron segments use to line them, the rapid early expansion of the London tube system would not have been possible. So effective was this means of construction that when, during the Second World War, the government needed quickly to provide large-scale air-raid shelters for the most vulnerable of the City's civilian population, and bomb-proof accommodation for its most crucial communications facilities, Greathead shields and segmented iron-ring construction were again employed.

As regards the transport element of this book, the essential point is not that a vast network of tunnels should have been built in a relatively short time-frame, but that so much of what was built was so quickly abandoned and is now hidden from public view. Subterranean London is littered with abandoned tube stations and the stub-ends of branch-lines that were never completed.

The reasons for this phenomenon are manifold, but two stand out. Some tube stations were simply ill-conceived, built as a result of over-optimistic traffic projections, or else constructed too close to existing stations that were more than adequate to handle both current and future passenger numbers. The second reason reflects the constantly changing demographic of Greater London and the fluctuations in traffic flows that this engenders. The population densities and travel patterns of different districts alter as previously slum residential areas become gentrified or are redeveloped for commercial use, while derelict industrial areas become new residential districts.

In the hands of property developers reacting to short economic cycles, such demographic changes occur quite rapidly in relation to the speed with which major changes to the city's transport infrastructure can be implemented. The results are a dearth of transport links in some areas and redundant facilities in others. This is not a purely historical phenomenon but one that was still to blight the city's transport planners as the twentieth century came to a close.

When the Jubilee Line was completed to Charing Cross in May 1979 it was expected that it would eventually be extended towards Lewisham via Aldwych. No one at that time anticipated the subsequent scale of the redevelopment of London's Dockland, and when it came about, the whole pattern of the Jubilee Line was recast. A new line was built from near Green Park via Westminster, Waterloo and Greenwich, terminating at Stratford. The platforms at Charing Cross, less than twenty years old, were abandoned.

War, or the threat of it, has had a profound effect upon the evolution of underground London. The topography of the lower Thames, the natural advantages of the estuary to facilitate shipping, and its proximity to its major trading partners on the European mainland ensured London's development as the country's principal commercial and maritime centre. It was inevitable that as London grew in stature as a centre of commerce it would also develop as a centre of government administration.

The natural advantages, however, are offset by serious strategic disadvantages. Historically, one of Britain's problems regarding the relationship between trade and defence has been that her principal trading partners have frequently also been, at one time or another, her enemies. Since the 1930s, when the major military threat to Britain shifted from attack by sea to attack from the air, London, situated close to the coast and at the narrow end of an estuary that acts like a direction-pointer to enemy aircraft, became exceptionally vulnerable.

The British government was acutely aware of this and by 1934, when another European war became a less than distant prospect, it took steps to evacuate many of the Capital's principal cultural institutions and its most important military and economic establishments to secure, remote locations in the provinces. Examples include the Army's war reserve of ammunition, transferred from Woolwich to Wiltshire, and

art treasures from London's museums and galleries evacuated first to remote country houses and thence to underground bunkers in North Wales and on the border of Somerset and Wiltshire.

Some of London's commercial and manufacturing capacity moved too, along with some of its people, but the majority stayed put. The pre-war population of London was approximately 8,500,000. At the war's end it was still a little over eight million and, during almost six years of conflict, measures were required to ensure their safety. A few huge, deep-level air-raid shelters were built (although, once completed, the government was in two minds as to whether they should actually be used), along with hundreds of smaller examples. Responsibility for the safety of civilians fell largely upon the local authorities through the medium of the Civil Defence and Air Raid Precautions organisations. All the London boroughs constructed bomb-proof control centres beneath their town halls or other civic properties, from which these services could be administered. Many still survive today in states of dereliction while others were secretly refurbished to serve a similar function in the event of a nuclear war with the Soviet Union.

Central government, too, sought safety underground during the Second World War and, like the majority of the population, demonstrated a marked reluctance to abandon central London, despite the risks involved. Early in the war a series of government bunkers were built in the northern suburbs but Churchill and the War Cabinet preferred to remain in Whitehall, beneath which a veritable warren of buried bunkers and communications centres were secretly constructed. Further from the city centre, but still within the orbit of this book, more underground bunkers, like those at Bentley Priory, Uxbridge and elsewhere, were built to protect the nerve centres of the military units that guarded London, and the country as a whole, against enemy attack. These too were subsequently upgraded to counter the new threats posed during the Cold War.

A little known, but important aspect of London's earlier industrial history is also covered in some depth. Most of the prestigious buildings we see now in London are built of Portland, Bath or Oxfordshire stone, but prior to the eighteenth century a more local stone was used. This was sourced principally from the Godstone, Merstham and Reigate areas where extensive underground quarries were developed over a period of two hundred years. Right up until the early 1960s quarries in this area were producing stone for a secondary use, as step-powder for whitening the doorsteps of the city's suburban homes.

Chapter 2

DISUSED TUBE STATIONS

The development of London's Underground Railways

By the second half of the nineteenth century, increasing urban congestion and the gradual drift of wealthier Londoners into the suburbs called for an improved transport system to cater for City of London workers. A system of underground passenger railways, which kept the streets clear for commercial goods traffic, was seen as the obvious solution and the first step towards developing such a system was the opening of the Metropolitan Railway in 1863. This was essentially a shallow sub-surface system constructed in cut-and-cover subways and joined the City at Smithfield to the developing suburbs of Middlesex via the mainline terminal stations at Paddington, Euston and Kings Cross. Meanwhile, in 1864, the Metropolitan District Railway sought to construct a similar line from South Kensington to Westminster and beyond. Construction of the first section was completed in 1868, with later extensions in the west to Fulham, Richmond, Ealing and Hounslow. Despite interminable disagreements, junctions were eventually made with the Metropolitan Railway in the west at Hammersmith and in 1884, following completion of an extension of the line eastwards, at Aldgate, to form a continuous route known as the Inner Circle.

Suburban expansion towards the end of the nineteenth century led to a rash of new proposals for underground passenger railways serving areas both north and south of the Thames. To avoid the disruption and cost associated with conventional cut-and-cover tunnelling techniques it was necessary to construct these railways as deep, bored tunnels at depths of between sixty and one hundred feet, a task made feasible by the presence at that depth of a stratum of relatively easily worked London clay, a material that readily lent itself to excavation by novel and speedy mechanical means. The first of these deep tube lines, opened in 1890, was the City & South London Railway which ran initially from Stockwell to Borough and thence under the Thames to King William Street in the City. Later, as we shall see, the line was extended south to Morden and the inconveniently positioned City terminus at King William Street

was abandoned. Subsequently a new spur, branching from the old City line at Borough, carried the route northwards through London Bridge, Bank and Angel and eventually, in the early decades of the twentieth century, on to Euston and Camden Town.

The Central London Railway, which later became the core of the Central Line, was first proposed in 1891 but difficulties in raising sufficient finance delayed construction and the first section of line, from Shepherd's Bush to Bank, was not opened to passengers until 30 July 1900. An extension westward to Wood Lane was completed in 1908 to provide facilities for the Franco-British Exhibition and Olympic Games which were held in London that year. In 1920 a short connecting link was made from Wood Lane station to join the Ealing and Shepherd's Bush line, operated by the Great Western Railway, allowing trains to run through to Ealing. A few years earlier, in 1912, the east end of the line had been extended to Liverpool Street.

The proprietors of the Baker Street & Waterloo Railway, the precursor of the Bakerloo Line, first applied for Parliamentary consent to build their line in 1891 but were plagued by financial obstacles and it was almost a decade before construction work began. Eventually, in 1897 sufficient funding was found via the London & Globe Finance Corporation, a somewhat dubious investment company controlled by J. Whitaker Wright. Within just a couple of years, however, Wright's financial empire had collapsed and in December 1900 he was facing charges of financial fraud. Found guilty in 1904 after a protracted trial, Wright took his own life using cyanide at the Royal Courts of Justice immediately after the verdict was announced. In the meantime, the Baker Street & Waterloo Railway had attracted the attention of an American railway entrepreneur, Charles Tyson Yerkes, of whom we will read much more below. Yerkes' financial probity was only marginally more ethical than Wright's, but under his guidance the Baker Street & Waterloo (and, indeed, several other ailing London underground railway projects), were brought to fruition. The line finally opened from a station at the junction of Melcolmbe Street and Dorset Square to Spur Road, Waterloo, on 10 March 1906.

Towards the end of the nineteenth century a number of railways were proposed to provide services from the northern suburbs into the City. Of these, two of the most important were the Brompton & Piccadilly Circus Railway, proposed in 1896, and the Great Northern & Strand Railway of 1898. Both companies, in common with the majority of London's underground railway schemes from the turn of the century, were chronically underfunded and made little material progress. Salvation eventually arrived in 1901 when both companies fell into the hands of Charles Tyson Yerkes who already had a financial interest in the Baker Street & Waterloo Railway and was a major shareholder of the Metropolitan District Railway. Under Yerkes the Brompton & Piccadilly Circus Railway was merged with the Great Northern & Strand Railway and authority obtained for the construction of an additional section of line to link the two railways between Piccadilly Circus and Brompton. At the same time, using Parliamentary powers obtained but never exercised for a proposed deep-level extension to the Metropolitan District Railway, (another Yerkes line), the route was extended to the southwest to join the Metropolitan District Railway at Hammersmith. To the north, the line terminated at the Great Northern & City Railway's terminus at Finsbury Park.

The line of the merged companies, now renamed the Great Northern, Piccadilly & Brompton Railway, opened to passengers on 15 December 1906. Prior to the merger the Great Northern & Strand Railway had planned to terminate its line at the Strand, but under the Yerkes scheme this was bypassed and instead the line continued through Holborn to Covent Garden, Leicester Square and beyond. Strand, however, was not forgotten and on 30 November 1907, just under a year after the completion of the main line, a shuttle service was inaugurated on a short branch line between Holborn and Strand (later renamed Aldwych to avoid confusion with another station on the underground system with the same name).

Another of the lines hoping to profit from the northward drift of London's commuter belt in the 1890s was the Hampstead, St. Pancras & Charing Cross Railway, which had been incorporated in November 1891 to construct a tube railway from Heath Street in Hampstead to the Strand near Charing Cross. Initially the proprietors encountered some Parliamentary opposition to its plans but eventually, in August 1893, the company, now renamed the Charing Cross, Euston & Hampstead Railway, received the necessary Royal Assent. Like the Baker Street & Waterloo and other railways under promotion at the same time, the Charing Cross,

Euston & Hampstead Railway encountered great difficulty in raising capital to finance its construction. Between 1894 and 1902 various amendments to the original Act were sought, either to extend the time period required for completion or for alterations to the route of the line, but in terms of material progress the scheme lay virtually dormant for almost ten years.

Once again, it was Charles Tyson Yerkes and his co-investors who came to the rescue, generating the capital required to allow construction to proceed. The line finally opened on 22 June 1907, with a main line running from Charing Cross to Camden Town and branches thence via Hampstead to Golders Green and to Highgate via South Kentish Town. In 1914 the line was extended south from Charing Cross to Embankment, and during the inter-war years the Golders Green branch was continued north to Edgware.

Charles Tyson Yerkes

As we have seen, the decade culminating in the death of Queen Victoria in January 1901 witnessed the birth of a plethora of imaginative schemes for tube railways to improve the speed of passenger transport and relieve the increasing congestion on the streets of London, but the cautious, risk-averse and conservative financial institutions that dominated the City of London at that time made the raising of capital to finance such innovative schemes virtually impossible via the conventional channels. We have seen too that, as in the case of Whitaker Wright, when British entrepreneurs adopted unconventional financing practices, the consequences tended towards catastrophe. Much of the impetus that led to the eventual construction of these lines was a consequence of the resourcefulness of Charles Tyson Yerkes, the American businessman disgraced in his own country, and to his capacity to attract foreign investment.

Yerkes was born near Philadelphia in 1837 and by 1865 was deeply involved in the notoriously corrupt American banking industry, dealing primarily in state and government bonds. In 1871 his ethically questionable business practices led to a short term of imprisonment for fraud. Following his release, Yerkes' attention turned to the financing of Chicago's urban transportation system and by the late 1880s he controlled the majority of the city's street railways. Increasingly frustrated in his Chicago business schemes, he transferred his operations in 1899 to New York. Shortly before the move to New York Yerkes was approached by two of the promoters of the Charing Cross, Euston & Hampstead Railway who were in

America on a desperate search for finance for their railway. Following a report from two of his subordinates, DeLancey Louderback and Henry Davis, who had been sent over to England to examine the prospects of the line, Yerkes visited London himself on 26 July 1900 and on 27 September acquired the undertaking. Shortly afterwards he also acquired a majority shareholding in the Metropolitan District Railway. Less than a year later Yerkes also purchased the Great Northern & Strand Railway and the Brompton & Piccadilly (subsequently amalgamated into the Great Northern, Piccadilly & Strand Railway), and in March 1902 made his final major acquisition, the half-completed Baker Street & Waterloo Railway.

The rapid rate of railway acquisitions, along with the cost of creating the Metropolitan District Electric Traction Company (essentially to fund the electrification of the Metropolitan District Railway and build the necessary electricity generating and distribution stations), meant that Yerkes' London operations were running perilously short of capital. To rectify the situation yet another company, The Underground Electric Railways Company of London Ltd, (UERL), was formed in April 1902 to raise sufficient funds through the medium of Speyer Brothers' banking house. The UERL was essentially a holding company that absorbed Yerkes' railway interests including the Metropolitan District, the Charing Cross, Euston & Hampstead, the Great Northern Piccadilly & Brompton and the Baker Street & Waterloo lines, along with the Metropolitan District Electric Traction Company. The UERL also acted as prime contractor for all construction work on the Yerkes lines, which resulted in the implementation of common standards throughout London's underground railway system.

Although the lines were now under the common umbrella of the UERL, the companies remained independent financial and legal entities, maintaining their own staff, operating procedures, ticketing arrangements and accounts management. In the face of stiff competition from London's omnibus and tram operators, this was clearly uneconomic and inefficient and, on 26 July 1910, in an effort to reduce overheads and streamline operational procedures and reduce tax liabilities, all the companies under the UERL umbrella were formally merged into a single company known as the London Electric Railway Company or LER. In 1913 the company completed its acquisitions (having already added the London General Omnibus Company to its portfolio in 1910) with the purchase of the remaining independent London tramway services along with the Central London Railway and the City & South London Railway, the latter undergoing reconstruction in the 1920s and incorporation into the Charing Cross, Euston & Hampstead Line to form a single entity that became the Northern Line. Yerkes did not live to witness the culmination of his London ambition, succumbing to kidney cancer in New York in 1905 at the age of sixty-eight.

In the years leading up to the First World War the group's omnibus and tram services made healthy profits that largely subsidised the less profitable underground railways. Unregulated competition in the immediate post-war years eroded these profits and threatened the viability of the entire passenger transport system of the Capital. Legislation was required to rectify the situation, the LER seeking government regulation and price control of transport services in the London area, statutory protection from competition and control of the London County Council tram system. After prolonged Parliamentary debate, however, government decided instead upon full public ownership. A Parliamentary bill was introduced in 1930 for the formation of a public corporation to take control of all the LER interests by means of a stock buy-out. The new controlling body, which came into existence on 1 July 1933, was known as the London Passenger Transport Board. The board was replaced by the London Transport Executive in 1948.

Trafalgar Square

The history of the tube stations in the Charing Cross area is a complex one, made more confusing by frequent changes of station name. In the early years of the twentieth century the mainline station was served by two separate underground railway companies. The Baker Street & Waterloo Railway (BS&WR), later to become the Bakerloo Line, opened its station, named Trafalgar Square, in March 1906. A year later, in 1907, the Charing Cross, Euston & Hampstead Railway (CCE&HR), later to become part of the Northern Line, opened its own station nearby naming it Charing Cross. For some years this was the southern terminus of the CCE&HR. By the time the stations became operational both railway companies had been absorbed into Yerkes' Underground Electric Railways of London, but despite their close proximity underground, the two stations had independent entrances and there was no interconnection for the convenience of passengers below ground. In 1914 the CCE&HR line was extended southwards beneath Charing Cross mainline station, where a new underground station was built, and onwards to form a junction with the BS&WR and the District Railway at Embankment station. Subsequently the former CCE&HR terminus, now a through station, was renamed Strand.

Strand station was closed on 4 June 1973 to facilitate the building of a new underground station serving Charing Cross on the Jubilee

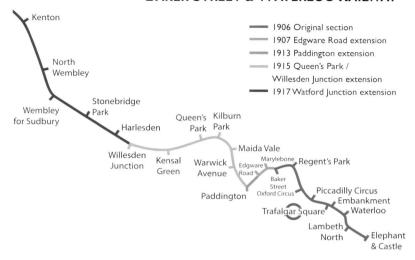

BAKER STREET & WATERLOO RAILWAY

— 1906 Original section
— 1907 Edgware Road extension
— 1913 Paddington extension
— 1915 Queen's Park / Willesden Junction extension
— 1917 Watford Junction extension

Line which was then under construction. The Jubilee Line platforms were squeezed in between the existing Bakerloo Line and Northern Line platforms and their construction led to a major reorganisation of underground facilities in the Charing Cross area. The Northern Line platforms were refurbished and interchange walkways provided for passengers between the old Northern and Bakerloo Line platforms and the new Jubilee Line platforms. The whole complex, including the former Trafalgar Square station, is now known as Charing Cross.

Above: The lower lift landing at Trafalgar Square. The walkway to the left of the photograph is relatively modern and spans the well of one of the disused lift shafts, joining the entry and exit sides of the landing.

Opposite left: A ventilation fan for the Bakerloo Line at the bottom of one of the former lift shafts. A small section of the distinctive bright green and golden brown tiling scheme can be seen on the wall of the passageway to the right of this picture.

Opposite right: The emergency exit staircase shaft at Trafalgar Square, now used only as an air inlet for the fan in the adjacent lift shaft. Notice the spiral pattern of green and brown tiles on the wall of the shaft, following the line of the now dismantled stairway

Wood Lane

The first section of the Central London Railway (CLR), later to become the Central Line, was opened between Shepherd's Bush and Liverpool Street on 30 July 1900. To the north of Shepherd's Bush, beyond the passenger station, the line continued for a short distance on a sharp incline to serve an extensive maintenance and repair yard

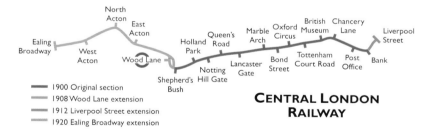

adjacent to the company's generating station. In July 1907 the CLR started work on a new station beyond Shepherd's Bush served by a single-line loop on the edge of their maintenance yard. The station carried the name Wood Lane and its function was to provide services for passengers visiting the 1908 Franco-British exhibition which was to be held on a 140-acre site on the west side of Wood Lane which would later become known as White City.

Some years later, under the joint proprietorship of the Great Western Railway and the Central London Railway, construction work began on the Ealing & Shepherd's Bush Railway, a westward extension of the CLR from Wood Lane to a terminus at Ealing

Broadway. Most of the work was completed by the early months of 1917, the first freight traffic moving over the line in April of that year. A full passenger service began on 3 August 1920. Two new cut-and-cover underground platforms were built at Wood Lane to serve the Ealing & Shepherd's Bush line, the westbound platform a little to the north of the existing station, the eastbound platform running beneath the station building.

The White City exhibition site became an increasingly popular event venue but it was soon evident that the existing Wood Lane station was inadequate to meet its needs. In 1938 Parliamentary consent was gained to move the station 350 yards north but the Second World War intervened and work on the new station, and realignment of the rails through the old Wood Lane station, did not begin until 1946. The new station, renamed White City, opened to passengers on 23 November 1947, the old station having closed on the previous day. Rails serving the high-level station were lifted in 1950 but trains entering the maintenance yard continued to run through the underground westbound platform 4. Eastbound service trains continued to run through the old underground platform 3 until it was finally demolished, along with Stanley Heaps' distinctive street-level booking hall, in 2005 during construction of the Westfield shopping centre. As part of the redevelopment a new, completely underground maintenance depot was constructed beneath the shopping centre. Meanwhile, in 2008, a new station named Wood Lane (not to be confused with the older, now demolished station on the Central London Railway), was opened on the Hammersmith & City line to serve the Westfield centre.

Above: The distinctive enamel London Transport 'roundel' station name boards like the example shown here in March 1980 were removed for preservation prior to the demolition of the station.

Opposite above: Stanley Heaps' distinctive entrance façade in 1996. One of the 'roundel' symbols and relief station name panels were recovered for restoration and display in London Transport Museum. The building was demolished during the construction of the Westfield London shopping centre which opened in October 2008.

Above: Posters dating from 1947 were still on display in the subway approaching platform 3 when this photograph was taken in February 1986.

Left: Distinctive green tiling in the long-disused subway linking platform 4 with platforms 1 and 2.

Above: Bound for Wood Lane depot, an empty Central Line train passes through the abandoned platform 4 in March 1980. Platform 4 was demolished during the construction of the Westfield shopping centre but Central Line passengers can still see the abandoned platform 3 from passing eastbound trains.

Left: A view looking north along platform 4. The platform was truncated at this point when the track giving access to Wood Lane depot was re-aligned in 1949.

North End – the station that never was

Parliamentary approval was granted for a tube line from Charing Cross to Hampstead in 1893, but due to difficulties in raising the necessary finance the scheme fell into abeyance until 1900 when the promoters, the Charing Cross & Hampstead Railway Company, were bought out by the American railway entrepreneur Charles Tyson Yerkes, whom we have met already in connection with a number of other underground ventures in London. Yerkes proposed to extend the line beneath Hampstead Heath to Golders Green, (much later it would continue on to Edgware as one of the northern extremities of the Northern Line), with the ulterior motive of exploiting the hitherto untouched farmland along the route for

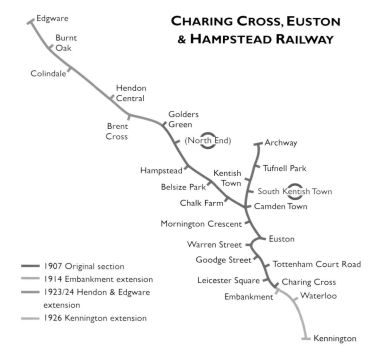

CHARING CROSS, EUSTON & HAMPSTEAD RAILWAY

— 1907 Original section
— 1914 Embankment extension
— 1923/24 Hendon & Edgware extension
— 1926 Kennington extension

housing development. Initially there was much opposition to this scheme but eventually, in 1903, Parliament relented and permission was granted. A provision of the Act was that, as extensive housing development now seemed inevitable, a station should be provided at North End, on the northern edge of Hampstead Heath, to meet the needs of the new residents who would otherwise be more-or-less marooned there. At 221 feet in depth, despite the line being on a rising gradient, North End (known as Bull & Bush in later

years on account of its proximity to the famous public house of that name) would have been the deepest station on the entire tube network.

Yerkes, however, found himself up against concerted resistance led by the formidable, and very wealthy, social activist and reformer Henrietta Octavia Barnett who, in conjunction with the architects Edwin Lutyens and Raymond Unwin, was at that time planning the model housing development of Hampstead Garden Suburb. Henrietta Barnett co-ordinated the purchase of much of the farmland at the northern end of Hampstead Heath which was later incorporated into the heath, guaranteeing its future in perpetuity. This scuppered Yerkes' own development plans and rendered North End station, where building work was already well under way, somewhat irrelevant. By the latter part of 1906 much of the excavation and underground building work for the station tunnels and connecting subways, up to the lower lift landing level, had been completed, but further work was then stopped before a start had been made on sinking the proposed lift shaft or erecting the surface building. Passenger services to Golders Green began on 22 June 1907, with trains passing the never-to-be-opened platforms at North End in darkness.

The Second World War & after

From 1933 operation of all the London tube lines was overseen from a control centre above Leicester Square station, and at the start of the Second World War an emergency control centre was constructed in a disused section of the station tunnels. Along with day-to-day train control, the emergency centre included facilities for the remote operation of a system of flood-gates in tube tunnels near the Thames that would be at risk of inundation if the tunnels were breached by enemy bombs. The installation of manually operated gates at some locations to safeguard against peace-time flooding had begun in the mid-1930s but the later installations, and the remote control facilities, were specific wartime precautions.

In 1953, as a consequence of the threat of an atomic war with the Soviet Union, plans were in preparation to increase the resilience of the tube network in order that it could survive operationally up to, and hopefully even beyond, attack by atomic weapons of similar magnitude to those deployed against the Japanese cities at the end of the Second World War. These plans involved the construction, away from the city centre, of bomb-proof traffic control facilities and a

Right: The site of the northbound platform, looking north towards Golders Green. Destined never to be used, the platform, completed in 1907, was cut back in the mid-1933 to avoid the risk of obstruction. The date of its final demolition is unknown. The area is now utilised for the storage of permanent way maintenance materials. A pile of new concrete sleepers can be seen in the middle distance.

remote control room for the flood-gates, including both the wartime gates and a comprehensive series of new ones currently under construction. The chosen location was the abandoned North End station which, as we have seen, was well away from the most vulnerable areas of the city at the deepest point on the entire tube system, and thus offered a remarkable level of protection. In 1954, on the edge of Hampstead Way near the now demolished Manor House Hospital, a small surface blockhouse was built above a new thirty-three-metre-deep vertical shaft containing a small lift and a spiral staircase to the proposed new control centre. Building work was begun in the area of the northbound platform to provide accommodation for the network operations centre while at a higher level, at the lower lift landing level, a two-storey control room was constructed to house, on the upper floor, the flood-gate control consoles and, on the lower floor, a battery and relay room. The flood control section was separated from the other facilities by a substantial blast door.

By 1955 however, by which time just the shell of the platform level offices had been completed, the advent of the Hydrogen bomb rendered most of the work redundant, the power of the new bomb being such that if London were attacked there would be no city, nor any trains, nor tunnels left to control. Work continued on the flood-gate control centre, however, as this still had an important peacetime emergency function to perform should, for example, unusual tidal or weather conditions cause the level of the Thames to rise quickly or should there be an accidental breach of one of the tunnels near the river. Although there was always some doubt about how effectively the flood-gate system would perform should an emergency arise, the control centre at North End was maintained up until 1984 when the commissioning of the Thames Barrier rendered it redundant. More recently, the station area has been used as a store for permanent way maintenance material and, like many other disused stations, acts as an emergency exit route for passengers should an incident occur in the tunnels.

Above: The formidable blast-proof entrance building above the lift and staircase shaft adjacent to Hampstead Way. This structure provided access to the flood-gate control centre below.

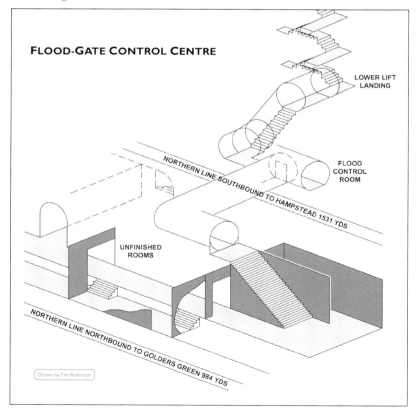

FLOOD-GATE CONTROL CENTRE

LOWER LIFT LANDING

NORTHERN LINE SOUTHBOUND TO HAMPSTEAD 1531 YDS

FLOOD CONTROL ROOM

UNFINISHED ROOMS

NORTHERN LINE NORTHBOUND TO GOLDERS GREEN 984 YDS

Drawn by Tim Robinson

Above: The bottom of the access shaft with the emergency stairway on the left and lift doors on the right. These are situated on the original CCE&HR station lower lift landing, twenty feet above rail level.
Below: The blast door sealing off the flood-gate control room from the rest of the North End emergency centre.

Above: The much vandalised flood-gate control panel at North End in 2009, twenty-five years after it was decommissioned. Compare this image with the black and white photograph on the following page. The steel door to the right of the two control positions gives access via a steel ladder to a battery and relay room on the floor below.

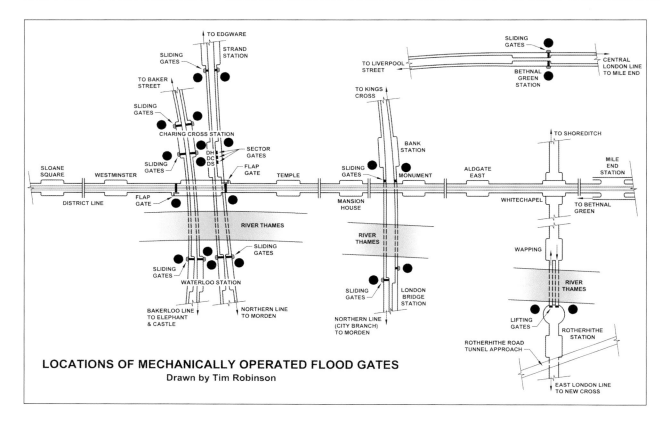

LOCATIONS OF MECHANICALLY OPERATED FLOOD GATES
Drawn by Tim Robinson

Left: Plan showing the locations of the post Second World War flood-gates.

Below left: Cross-sectional elevation of a lifting flood-gate of the type installed at Rotherhithe. Under normal operating conditions the gate is raised into a recess in the tunnel roof.

Below right: This photograph of the flood-gate control panel was taken while the control centre was operational. The left-hand panel was transferred from the earlier operations room at Leicester Square and operates the series of gates installed during the Second World War. The right-hand panel operates the post-war system of gates. Each gate can be controlled independently or the whole system can be opened or closed simultaneously by means of the master control levers at the bottom of the panel.

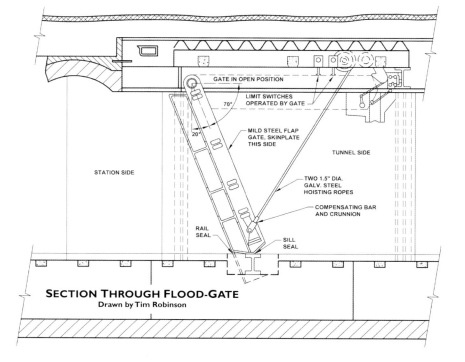

SECTION THROUGH FLOOD-GATE
Drawn by Tim Robinson

Above: Part of the section of station tunnel originally constructed to house the northbound platform was reconfigured in the early 1950s to accommodate London Transport's proposed emergency network control centre but, in 1955, work on this project was brought to a halt as the nature of the perceived threat to the capital's infrastructure underwent a radical reappraisal with the advent of nuclear weapons. This view shows the unfinished shell of the office complex with the wall to the right following the line of the former platform edge and forming a barrier between the offices and the tube running line beyond.

Above: The remains of the southbound platform at North End. The steps to the left of this photograph, fitted with modern handrails, give access to the stairway in the former flood-gate control centre's access shaft via the original CCE&HR subway, which acts as an emergency exit for passengers or crew in the event of a train failure in the tunnel.

Left: The frontage of South Kentish Town station, built in red-glazed brick to a typical Leslie Green design, facing onto Kentish Town Road. The adjacent Castle public house, which gave its name to nearby Castle Street, was renamed 'The Flowerpot' in recent years and was a popular live music venue until its closure in 2011.

South Kentish Town

Between Kentish Town and Camden Town stations on the Northern Line there stands the remains of South Kentish Town station, recognisable now from passing trains as little more than a brief widening of the tunnels. Opened on 22 June 1907 along with all the other stations on the former Charing Cross, Euston & Hampstead Railway, South Kentish Town was at first planned to be called Castle Road. For reasons unrecorded, the name was changed to South Kentish Town shortly before the opening ceremony, but not before the underground platforms had been emblazoned 'Castle Road' in glazed enamel tiles. These were subsequently painted over and the new name substituted in a rather more prosaic style. The station, lying fifty feet below ground and designed by the architect Leslie Green, was accessed by a pair of electric lifts in a single, twenty-three-foot diameter vertical shaft. A narrower, eighteen-foot diameter shaft was fitted with a spiral staircase to provide an emergency exit route.

From very early days it was obvious that traffic was not going to meet expectations and just a year after opening many trains were scheduled to pass South Kentish Town without stopping. An unofficial strike by workers at Lots Road power station, which generated electricity for the lines of the London Electric Railway Company, led to the temporary closure of tube stations throughout the capital in June 1924. At the end of the industrial action the decision was taken not to reopen South Kentish Town and nearby Mornington Crescent stations, both of which were deemed uneconomical. A month later, on 2 July 1924, Mornington Crescent was granted a reprieve and the station remains in service today, relieving the pressure on the increasingly busy nearby Camden Town station. South Kentish Town, however, never re-entered service.

Like City Road, the disused underground platforms at South Kentish Town were used as an air-raid shelter during the Second World War. Subsequently the platforms were demolished although a new staircase has been erected in the former lift shaft for use as an escape route for passengers should an emergency occur in the tunnels, and as an access point for permanent way maintenance staff. Only the supporting ironwork for the original spiral staircase now survives in the small emergency exit shaft which is sealed at the top by a concrete cap.

Above: The site of the northbound platform at South Kentish Town with the bridge carrying the passenger subway across the track to the station's lower lift landing. The pattern of the original dark red and cream is clearly visible in this photograph although it has been painted over and is further obscured by a dense layer of dust.

Opposite: The site of the southbound platform at South Kentish Town. Like the northbound station tunnel (and several other disused stations on the London Underground) this area is now used for the storage of track maintenance equipment. The bright light visible in the running tunnel in the background is a reflection from the headlight of an approaching train.

Above left: The base of one of the disused lift shafts at South Kentish Town, now fitted with a ventilation fan and associated trunking. The abandoned station functions as an emergency exit point for passengers aboard trains that come to grief in the tunnels; the modern spiral steel staircase visible in this photograph provides the emergency route to the surface.

Above Right: The original emergency exit staircase shaft, now sealed by a concrete slab at the surface. Only the main supporting girder for the staircase has survived although its position is marked by the spiral incision in the wall of the shaft.

Right: The lifts at South Kentish Town were double-sided with landings and access subways on each side. Following closure the landing visible in this photograph was not incorporated in the emergency exit route and is used only for ventilation purposes.

Opposite: A view from inside the disused lift shaft looking out onto the lower lift landing.

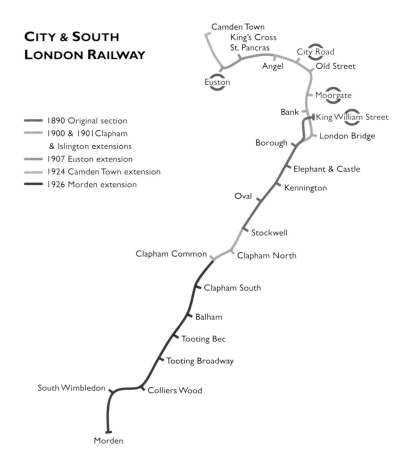

CITY & SOUTH LONDON RAILWAY

— 1890 Original section
— 1900 & 1901 Clapham & Islington extensions
— 1907 Euston extension
— 1924 Camden Town extension
— 1926 Morden extension

Camden Town
King's Cross
St. Pancras
City Road
Angel
Old Street
Euston
Moorgate
Bank
King William Street
London Bridge
Borough
Elephant & Castle
Kennington
Oval
Stockwell
Clapham Common
Clapham North
Clapham South
Balham
Tooting Bec
Tooting Broadway
South Wimbledon
Colliers Wood
Morden

Euston

The City & South London Railway opened an underground station serving Euston on 12 May 1907 following the completion of the westward extension of their line from Moorgate. The station's Moorish-style surface building by the architect Sidney Smith, containing a booking hall and lifts to the underground platforms, was located on the corner of Eversholt Street and Doric Way. Meanwhile, the Charing Cross, Euston & Hampstead Railway (CCE&HR), after initially and rather foolishly deciding to bypass Euston on their Charing Cross to Golders Green line, changed their plans and belatedly provided a station at Euston, a little to the west of the mainline terminus on the corner of Drummond Street, which opened to passengers on 22 June 1907. The CCE&HR surface building was a typical example of the glazed terracotta elevations designed for the company by Leslie Green.

Deep below ground the two stations, owned and operated by

different companies, were in quite close proximity so an agreement was reached for a connecting passage to be built between them allowing the interchange of passengers between lines without the inconvenience of having to go to the surface and walk between ticket offices located some distance apart. To facilitate this a small interchange ticket office was established in the connecting passage. Shortly afterwards new lift shafts were sunk and a sub-surface booking hall built beneath the concourse of Euston mainline station giving access via the lifts and a pair of deep-level walkways from the lower lift landing to both the CCE&HR and C&SLR platforms. Briefly, all three access points continued in service but soon the operating companies realised that this was an expensive extravagance and the original surface buildings at Eversholt Street and Drummond Street were closed.

The next major alterations to the underground stations at Euston began in 1967 with the rebuilding of the mainline station construction of the Victoria Line. The purpose of the Victoria Line was to relieve pressure on other sections of the tube system and, to ease the flow of passengers, it was intended that wherever possible cross-platform interchanges should be facilitated. At Euston the new Victoria Line platforms are situated between the southbound and realigned northbound platforms of the former C&SLR (now the Northern Line City Branch) station. The original C&SLR station had a dangerously narrow island platform, so when the station was reconstructed the existing southbound platform was retained and extended across the northbound line, which was taken out of use. The northbound rails were then diverted over and to the south of the Victoria Line through a newly constructed tunnel and a new platform built parallel with and to the south of the Victoria Line platforms. At the same time the booking hall beneath the mainline station was rebuilt and provided with two sets of escalators down to an intermediate circulating area. From there further escalators descend to the Northern Line City Branch platforms and the former CCE&HR (now the Northern Line Charing Cross Branch) stations. The new station came into use on 11 December 1969 after which most of the original linking passageways were blocked off except where they were required for ventilation.

Above left: The surface building for the CCE&HR Euston station on the corner of Drummond Street has been disused since 1913 and now functions as a ventilation duct; hence the open mesh grilles that now fill the former semi-circular window openings adjacent to the road junction.

Above right: The capped emergency staircase shaft at Drummond Street. The pattern of spiral tiling and the cut-outs in the wall of the shaft that once supported the outer ends of the stair treads are clearly visible.

Left: The lower lift landing of the new, combined station entrance on the concourse of Euston mainline terminus which was opened in 1915 when the C&SLR and CCE&HR underground stations were connected via a passenger subway. The lifts were taken out of use in 1969 during the construction of the Victoria Line.

EUSTON STATION

**SHOWING INTERCHANGE,
TICKET OFFICE,
SUBWAYS & LIFTS**

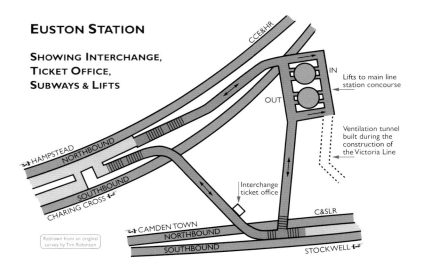

Right: Detail view of the ticket window at the interchange ticket office.

Below: This view, looking towards the former CCE&HR station, shows the location of the ticket office in the now disused interchange subway.

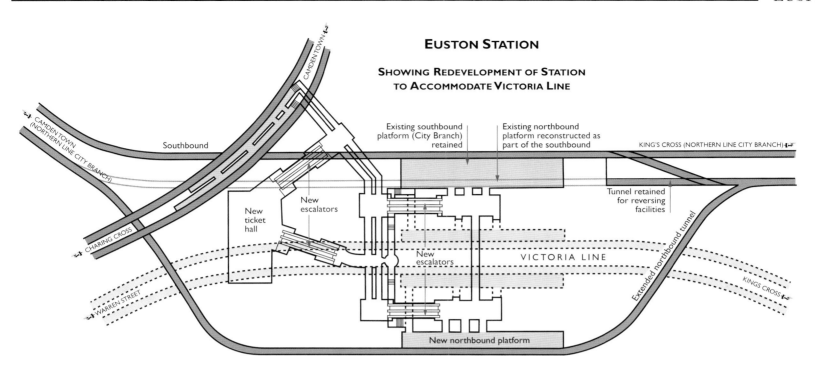

EUSTON STATION

SHOWING REDEVELOPMENT OF STATION TO ACCOMMODATE VICTORIA LINE

CAMDEN TOWN

CAMDEN TOWN (NORTHERN LINE CITY BRANCH)

Southbound

Existing southbound platform (City Branch) retained

Existing northbound platform reconstructed as part of the southbound

KING'S CROSS (NORTHERN LINE CITY BRANCH)

CHARING CROSS

New ticket hall

New escalators

Tunnel retained for reversing facilities

New escalators

VICTORIA LINE

Extended northbound tunnel

WARREN STREET

KINGS CROSS

New northbound platform

Above: Schematic layout diagram showing the alterations made to the Northern Line City Branch platforms at Euston during the construction of the Victoria Line. Note that the Victoria Line has right-hand running at Euston.

Left: The surviving stub-end of the original northbound platform of the Northern Line City Branch at Euston. The steel staircase to the right of the photograph gave access to a high-level signal cabin that was taken out of use in 1958. The cabin still retains a signalling function, however, as it now serves as a remote interlocking machine room.

Above: The crossover tunnel to the east of the southbound City Line platform at Euston. The line to the left is the southbound running line with a crossover linking to the former northbound line. The latter connects to the new extended northbound line and from there with the Kings Cross Loop to allow stock interchange between the Northern and Piccadilly lines. The tunnel only partially visible in the far right background housed a seven-car siding used to reverse trains terminating at Euston. This was taken out of use in 1967 and the rails subsequently lifted. The rail in the foreground is the short surviving section of the former northbound City Line.

City Road

City Road station, located between Old Street and Angel on what is now the Northern Line, was opened for traffic on 17 November 1901 as part of the northward extension of City & South London Railway (C&SLR) from Moorgate Street. Designed by the architect Thomas Phillips Figgis, the station, which was accessed by a single vertical shaft containing two lifts, was sixty-five feet below ground and consisted of two parallel station tunnels and interconnecting walkways. Located in an economically deprived area of London and situated too close to the much more conveniently positioned Old Street and Angel stations, City Road was never heavily patronised and its closure was contemplated from as early as 1908.

In January 1913 the C&SLR was absorbed into the near-monopoly of the Underground Electric Railway Company of London (UERL) and in 1922 the parent company began a programme of engineering works to enlarge the sizes of the station and running tunnels of the former C&SLR to those of the more recently constructed underground electric system. Following completion of the work in April 1924 the line was re-opened but City Road remained shut; the paucity of passengers had made enlargement work there uneconomic and it was decided that the station should be permanently closed and dismantled. The platforms and both lifts were subsequently removed and the lift shaft adapted for ventilation purposes, the upper section of the shaft being extended for this purpose above the roof-line of the surface buildings.

In the early years of the Second World War, City Road was earmarked for use as an air-raid shelter for 449 persons. Six-foot-high brick walls were constructed along what would have been the position of the platform edges to protect shelterers from passing trains and a spiral staircase erected for access in the existing vertical shaft. Toilets were established in the passageway linking the lower lift landing to the southbound platform, at the north end of which a canteen was constructed. A first aid post was built on the northbound platform. The shelter came into use in the early weeks of 1942 but the whole site was quickly cleared at the end of the war and little trace now remains. Most of the surface buildings associated with the station, other than the tall brick ventilation tower, were demolished in the early 1970s. New electric lighting has been installed underground together with a steel stairway in the shaft to provide an emergency exit from trains stranded in the tunnel. The area previously occupied by the platforms is now used as a permanent way store.

Above: City Road station building in 1967. Photo courtesy of J.E. Connor.

Below: Steps leading up from rail level to the lower lift landing. The steel treads bridge the gap from the original stairway left when the platform was demolished. These provide an emergency exit route, via a new spiral steel staircase in the disused lift shaft, allowing passengers to detrain in the tunnel in case of emergency.

Above: The site of the northbound platform at City Road, now used as a dumping ground for permanent way maintenance materials. The arched openings of the cross passages linking the northbound and southbound platforms can be seen in the left-hand wall of the station tunnel.

Left: One of the two landings at the top of the emergency staircase shaft from the former City & South London station at Moorgate, disused since 1924 when the lifts were replaced by escalators. The subway behind the photographer's position once led to the sub-surface Metropolitan Line platform but is now blocked by a concrete barrier.

Moorgate

The modernisation of Moorgate during the years 1922-1924 and an aborted short extension of the Great Northern & City Line to Lothbury resulted in a number of disused, abandoned passageways and one particularly fascinating, hidden feature of considerable historical significance.

The City & South London Railway (C&SLR), having decided to abandon its original terminus at King William Street, was extended first to Moorgate Street, which opened in February 1900, then to a new station at Angel, which came into service on 11 May 1907, and eventually on to Euston. This route was later to become the City Branch of the Northern Line. Following its absorption into Charles Tyson Yerkes' Underground Electric Railways of London company, plans were prepared in 1914 to reconstruct the tunnels of the C&SLR to the same standard as Yerkes' other London tube railways. The First World War intervened, however, and the upgrade was not started until August 1922. The line was temporarily closed for the next two years while the tunnels were widened and, as at Moorgate, escalators installed to replace the earlier lifts. Here, the redundant lift shafts, lower lift landing and associated passageways were retained

for ventilation purposes. These still survive in their more-or-less original form, although closed off from public view.

At the turn of the nineteenth century, the Great Northern & City Railway (GN&CR) proposed an underground line from Finsbury Park to Moorgate running in large diameter tunnels capable of accommodating mainline locomotives and rolling stock. The Great Northern Railway, however, (the main sponsors of the GN&CR) were not keen on the scheme and the project languished. Undeterred, the GN&CR ploughed on and in November 1901 sought a Parliamentary Bill to extend their line a further 270 yards beyond Moorgate to a new terminus at Lothbury. The extension was authorised in February 1902 but with funds difficult to raise the extension was abandoned, although not until a short section of the southbound tunnel had been excavated beyond the end of the station at Moorgate. The line eventually opened from Finsbury to Moorgate in February 1904. Two further attempts to revive the extension scheme were made in 1907 and 1913 but neither came to fruition. The Greathead tunnelling shield, left in the uncompleted southbound tunnel in 1903 when it was thought that it might still be required to complete the extension is still in position, abandoned and virtually forgotten.

Above left: A view looking up one of the disused lift shafts at Moorgate with the portals of the upper lift landings clearly visible on the left-hand side. A modern ventilation duct protrudes from one of the portals.

Above right: The lower lift landing, showing the shaft lining and, on the left, the tiled subway leading to the platforms.

Left: The bottom of the second lift shaft now functions as a machine room housing ventilation plant. The steel stairway in the left foreground leads down to a short walkway giving access to one of the Northern Line running tunnels.

Opposite: One of London Transport's most important hidden treasures: the Greathead tunnelling shield that has lain abandoned in the aborted Great Northern & City Line Lothbury extension tunnel at Moorgate since 1903.

Above: A view of the Great Northern & City Line platform 10 at Moorgate, seen from the bridge to Moorgate sub-station that spans the abandoned extension to Lothbury. The Greathead shield seen on the previous page is immediately behind the photographer.

King William Street

King William Street station was the City terminus of the City & South London Railway (C&SLR) which has the distinction of being the world's first deep-level underground electric railway, carrying commuters from south of the Thames via stations at Borough, Elephant & Castle, Kennington, Oval and Stockwell. The inconvenience of the King William Street terminus was apparent from the start. From Borough station the line passed beneath the Thames just west of London Bridge negotiating a series of steep gradients before turning sharply to the east on the approach to the rather cramped single-line platform. The situation was eased slightly in 1895 when the station was reconfigured with an island platform having a running line on each side, but this was only a partial palliative. The inconvenient location of King William Street hampered the ambition of the C&SLR to extend northward to Moorgate and beyond, while the lack of a station north of Borough at London Bridge deprived the company of potentially lucrative traffic to and from the mainline station there.

A Parliamentary Bill was put forward in 1892 to allow construction of the first stage of the northern extension of the C&SLR but approval was delayed for four years. Work on the extension eventually started in 1896 but on a plan much altered from that originally proposed. A new line was to be constructed branching east from Borough via a new station at London Bridge, passing under the Thames east of the bridge before heading north towards Bank and Moorgate. The tunnels from Borough to King William Street were abandoned and the old City terminus was closed on 25 February 1900. The rails were left in situ for some years and were used as empty-stock storage sidings but in 1914, at the start of the First World War, the twin tunnels under the Thames were sealed off as it was thought they posed a security risk. The surface booking hall and company offices at No. 46 King William Street were demolished in 1933 to make way for Regis House, a new office development. This in turn was demolished in 1995 to be replaced by a modern office block also known, somewhat confusingly, as Regis House.

The abandoned tunnels and station emerged from obscurity as two separate entities at the start of the Second World War. The disused tunnels running from the abandoned junction at Borough towards the Thames were leased by Southwark Borough Council in January 1940 at an annual rent of £100 and the section that ran beneath Borough High Street was converted into an air-raid shelter

for 8,000 people. Estimates for the work were prepared by Mott, Hay and Anderson, a firm of consulting engineers that had worked closely with the London Passenger Transport Board (LPTB) and its predecessors, and who were to remain involved in a number of subterranean projects for the British Government during the post-war years. The conversion work was carried out by Kinnear, Moodie & Company, who also had considerable past experience with the LPTB. Previous to this, as a consequence of the Munich Crisis in October 1938, concrete bulkheads had been built across the tunnels near the Borough junction and at a point just south of the river, the latter bulkhead being fitted with a substantial watertight door. A third pair

Below: One of several wartime posters that survived until recent years in the King William Street shelter. Alterations to the ventilation system subsequently resulted in very rapid decay.

Left: The upper floor of the King William Street shelter with what appears to be toilet cubicles at the far end.

of bulkheads was built north of the river across the station approach tunnels. Six discrete entrance shafts were constructed to the rear of buildings along Borough High Street, in Marlborough Yard and in the garden of St. George's church in Tabard Street. Within the tunnels concrete slab floors were laid and electric lighting, benches and several blocks of toilets were installed. In the former down-line tunnel, near the Borough bulkhead, Southwark Council constructed a strongroom for the safe keeping of the municipal archives and other valuable artefacts during the wartime years. In recent years the tunnels were broken through during the construction of the Jubilee Line, while at the point where the old tunnels cross London Bridge station they have been adapted for ventilation purposes.

The wartime history of the station tunnels was somewhat different. At the start of the war, Regis House was occupied by a number of businesses including the United Dominions Trust. The surface building was adapted for commercial use and the seventy-five-foot vertical lift shaft, bereft of its two hydraulic lifts which had been removed shortly after closure, were infilled. The smaller emergency staircase, however, was still open and accessible from the basement of Regis House, which had once been the station booking hall. In November 1939 the owners of Regis House arranged a lease on the underground station area and the crossover tunnels leading to the bulkhead north of the Thames and fitted it out as a private air-raid shelter. Within the station tunnel a mezzanine floor was constructed, effectively doubling the floor area available. At the same time a new, sixty-four-foot-deep shaft was sunk from the basement of King William House, another office block on the opposite side of King William Street from Regis House, terminating underground at the end of the crossover tunnel at the end of the station, just before the rails diverged into their separate up and down line running tunnels. The shelter could accommodate 2,000 workers from the two office buildings and was provided with both dormitory accommodation and office space so that at least some staff members could work through the raids. Space was found on the mezzanine floor for an air-conditioning and ventilation plant and two toilet blocks, one male and one female were built in the ends of the running tunnels.

Unfortunately, construction of the air-raid shelter wiped away most of the distinctive features of the C&SLR station although a little of the original tiling has survived in one location. After the war the lease on the station was extended, certainly up until the mid-1970s when it was utilised by the owners of Regis House as a document store.

Above: One of the lower-floor shelter rooms at King William Street. The upper floor, access to which is gained via the wooden staircase visible in the background, is supported by substantial steel girders. The door to the left of this photograph opens onto an access corridor that runs the full length of the shelter.

Above: The base of the staircase shaft built during WW2 to give access to the shelter from King William Street House, now securely sealed.

Below: Surviving original tile-work at the east end of the lower-floor shelter room and in the pedestrian passage beyond.

Above: Gentlemen's toilet cubicles in the southbound running tunnel.

Below: An ancillary room at King William Street, one of the few areas in the former station that retains all of its original C&SLR tiling intact.

Above: The northbound running tunnel at King William Street, beyond the female toilets, with the concrete bulkhead and sealed door beneath Upper Thames Street visible in the background.

GREAT NORTHERN, PICCADILLY & BROMPTON RAILWAY

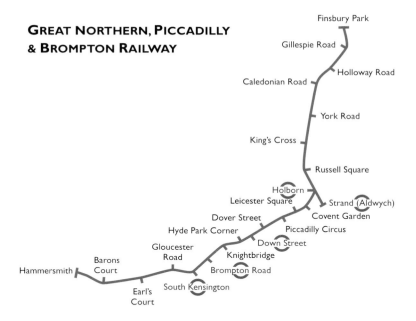

Aldwych & Holborn

The Great Northern & Strand Railway was to have terminated at the Strand, but under Yerkes' scheme this was dropped and instead the line continued south and west via Holborn, Covent Garden, Leicester Square and on towards Hammersmith. A short, twin-tunnel branch was opened from Holborn to Strand in November 1907, the construction of Strand station having begun on the site of the recently demolished Royal Strand Theatre on 21 October 1905. To avoid confusion with a similarly named station on the Charing Cross, Euston & Hampstead Railway, Strand was renamed Aldwych in 1915. Initially, consideration was given to extending this branch to Temple and Waterloo. This was not proceeded with although the scheme has been briefly revisited several times over the ensuing ninety-seven years. Most recently a costed scheme was prepared to extend the Docklands Light Railway (DLR) through Aldwych to join the now disused Jubilee Line platforms at Charing Cross which would be adapted to accommodate DLR trains.

The station's surface building, with typical red-glazed terracotta frontages by the architect Leslie Green on Strand and Surrey Street, stands ninety-two feet six inches above the underground platforms. In anticipation of the possible extension to Waterloo some of the facilities at Aldwych were lavish, although the platforms were somewhat shorter than at other Great Northern, Piccadilly & Brompton Railway (GNP&BR) stations. Three lift shafts were

constructed to house a total of six electric lifts but, because the extension was never completed, only one of the shafts ever had lifts installed. A smaller, fourth vertical shaft contained an emergency spiral staircase. Two sets of stairways were constructed from the platforms connected via intermediate passages to the front and rear lift landings but, again due to the non-completion of the intended extension, the set at the end of the platform furthest from Holborn was left in an uncompleted state, their access routes blocked by barriers.

The Holborn to Aldwych branch was operated as a self-contained unit with a shuttle train running in to what were effectively bay platforms (platforms 5 and 6) at Holborn, although the eastern line continued on past the Holborn platforms to connect with the eastbound GNP&BR main line via trailing points. This connection was not generally used for passenger traffic, (although sparsely patronised through trains from Finsbury Park for theatre-goers were run until 1908), but facilitated stock movement when necessary. In 1917 the bay platform (platform 5) at Holborn and the eastern of the two lines of the branch were closed and the tracks removed. Thereafter the single-car shuttle ran on the western track from Aldwych, through what had been a crossover beyond the platform ends before terminating at platform 6 at Holborn.

From 1917 the disused eastern platform at Aldwych was used by the National Gallery for the safe storage of some of its pictures and other artefacts in the wake of German aerial bombardment of the city. In June 1938 the Museums and Galleries Air Raid Precaution Committee, a body formed four years earlier to plan the safeguarding of treasures from London's museums and galleries during the next European war which even at that early date the strategists viewed as inevitable, reached an agreement for the use of Aldwych station as a repository in the event of war. Consequently, shortly after the outbreak of the Second World War, passenger services were suspended and the station was occupied by the Public Records Office and the British Museum for the secure storage of documents, archives and artefacts. Much of the British Museum's contents had already been evacuated to a number of remote country houses far from the perceived danger areas; some, for example, had gone to the Duke of Buccleuch's Boughton House estate in Northamptonshire while many of the smaller items including the collection of coins and medals went to Skipton Castle. Larger, less easily transportable items including the Elgin Marbles and other statuary from the Greek and Roman department found their way to Aldwych, transported to the

Above: Leslie Green's restrained frontage for Strand (later Aldwych) station after closure.

station on a scheduled late-night ballast train from Lillie Bridge maintenance yard to where they had been delivered by lorry earlier in the evening. At Aldwych they were joined by other items of massive monumental masonry and metalwork from elsewhere around the city, including Francis Derwent Wood's monument to the Machine Gun Corps from Hyde Park Corner.

As the war progressed, neither Sir John Forsdyke, Director and Principal Librarian of the British Museum, who had overseen the evacuation, nor the Ministry of Home Security, were entirely happy with the arrangement. Forsdyke was not convinced that the station was sufficiently secure against the threat of sustained bombardment, while the Ministry had alternative designs upon the site. In September 1940 Westminster City Council had been allowed occupancy of parts of the platforms at Aldwych and some 320 yards of running tunnels for use as an air-raid shelter to relieve pressure on a similar shelter at Holborn. The following March a concerted press campaign brought pressure upon the museum to make more space available for shelter use, highlighting as scandalous the fact that public money was being frittered on safeguarding what were described as 'elitist trifles' while the city's population was left to fend for itself amongst the bombs. There was, too, another reason for concern; walls constructed to partition the adjacent air-raid shelter restricted air flow in the section of tunnel used by the British Museum and, in consequence, the heightened humidity encouraged the growth of mould and the physical deterioration of the more delicate artefacts stored there. Over the following weeks most of the residual museum material was transferred to Skipton Castle, only to be moved again a few

months later to a disused underground stone quarry at Westwood in Wiltshire where it joined all the other artefacts from the London museums and galleries previously dispersed to remote country houses in the provinces. The fall of France in the spring of 1940 and the subsequent occupation by the Luftwaffe of airfields on the Channel coast rendered the previously secure country house repositories, invulnerable due to their remoteness, at serious risk from German bombers that could now range over the whole of Britain.

All that remained at Aldwych were the Elgin Marbles and a few other heavy items of statuary, most of which were returned to the museum in early April 1946, three months before passenger services were reinstated. Due to damage caused by enemy bombing to the new Duveen Gallery, which was specially designed to house the Elgin Marbles at the British Museum and upon which work had begun in 1938 but which remained unfinished at the outbreak of war, the Marbles remained in store at Aldwych until 25 November 1948. It is perhaps ironic that the original Greek and Roman gallery which had previously housed them before the war, albeit under somewhat unsatisfactory conditions, survived the war unscathed. The rebuilt Duveen Gallery was not completed until 1962.

Meanwhile, the disused platform 5 and its adjoining track-bed at Holborn were converted into emergency office accommodation. Single-storey offices were built on the platform with a narrow corridor along the platform edge, while on the track-bed, making use of the extra headroom available, a range of two-storey offices and dormitories was constructed with the dormitories on the upper floor. More than fifty offices were squeezed into the available space including a GPO telephone exchange and a further switchboard connected to the London Passenger Transport Board telephone system. In the immediate post-war years the offices were utilised as temporary hostel accommodation for LPTB staff who had been rendered homeless due to enemy action. In more recent years the complex has been used as workshop and storage space by the University of London.

Passenger services were finally withdrawn from the Aldwych branch in 1994. Currently parts of the station are used for testing new lighting, facias, tiling and platform furniture before being rolled out onto the wider London underground system. The branch, including platforms 6 at Holborn and 1 at Aldwych, together with the recently restored surface ticket office, is frequently used as a period set for film and television, a train of Northern Line 1972 stock being permanently positioned in the station for this purpose.

HOLBORN STATION

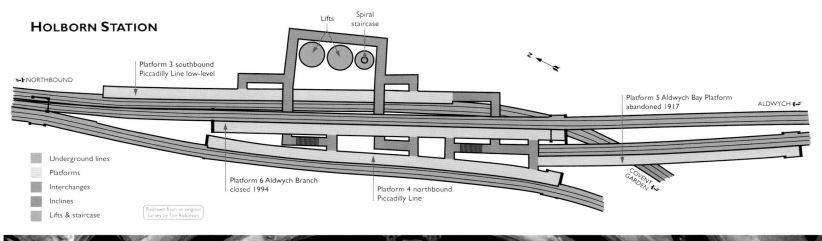

NORTHBOUND

Lifts

Spiral staircase

Platform 3 southbound
Piccadilly Line low-level

Platform 5 Aldwych Bay Platform
abandoned 1917

ALDWYCH

Underground lines

Platforms

Interchanges

Inclines

Lifts & staircase

Platform 6 Aldwych Branch
closed 1994

Platform 4 northbound
Piccadilly Line

COVENT GARDEN

Redrawn from an original
survey by Tim Robinson

Above: A view north along platform 6 at Holborn, towards Russell Square station.
Notice the safety link between the power rails on the Aldwych branch track.

Right: The south end of platform 6 at Holborn with the eastern running tunnel to Aldwych in the background. The glazed wooden structure on the platform is the former Aldwych branch signalbox.

Below: The crossover tunnel to the south of Holborn station on the Aldwych branch. The western running tunnel, taken out of use in 1917, is to the left of this photograph, its entrance in the headwall now blocked by a brick wall and small pedestrian door. At this point the track in the western tunnel, which formerly served bay platform 5 at Holborn, crosses to the alignment of the eastern tunnel to enter platform 6, allowing through running for stock transfers on the Piccadilly Line.

Above: Surviving wartime offices and dormitories on platform 5 at Holborn in 1995. The alignment of the platform edge can be seen in the centre of the corridor. Due to the additional height available from rail level on the right-hand side, it was possible to build dormitories above the offices there. Wooden stairs to the upper floor can be seen through the door.

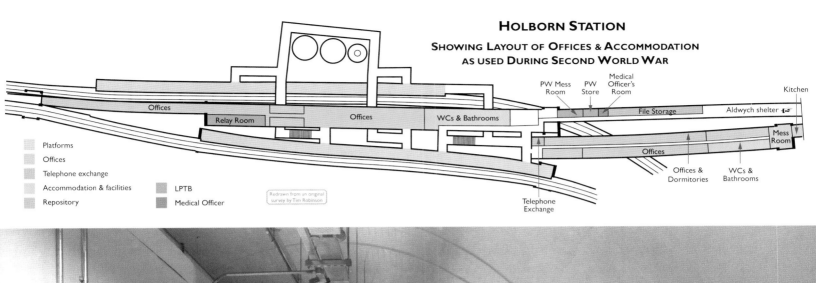

HOLBORN STATION

SHOWING LAYOUT OF OFFICES & ACCOMMODATION AS USED DURING SECOND WORLD WAR

Offices

Relay Room

Offices

WCs & Bathrooms

PW Mess Room

PW Store

Medical Officer's Room

File Storage

Aldwych shelter

Kitchen

Offices

Mess Room

Platforms

Offices

Telephone exchange

Accommodation & facilities

Repository

LPTB

Medical Officer

Redrawn from an original survey by Tim Robinson

Telephone Exchange

Offices & Dormitories

WCs & Bathrooms

Top: Plan showing the wartime layout of office and hostel accommodation at Holborn.

Above: The same location in 2008. The offices to the left of the central passageway have been refurbished while the dormitories to the right have been demolished to provide a larger circulating area.

ALDWYCH STATION

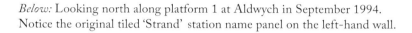

Right: The eastern running tunnel looking from Aldwych towards Holborn. During the Second World War this was utilised as an air-raid shelter.

Below: Looking north along platform 1 at Aldwych in September 1994. Notice the original tiled 'Strand' station name panel on the left-hand wall.

Left: The shuttle train waiting at platform 1 at Aldwych in September 1992.

Below left: Aldwych station nameplate and notice of closure poster, October 1992.

Below right: The end of the line … buffer stops at Aldwych, August 2005.

Right: Cause for confusion – following closure, platform 2 at Aldwych was used by London Transport as a testing-ground for new designs of station furniture, signage, décor and lighting. Here we see an experimental installation of name panels for Holborn. After the lifts at Aldwych were taken out of use the experimental work was transferred to platform 6 at Holborn.

Left: Not a feature of the Aldwych branch, but interesting nevertheless; this is an interior view of the small signal cabin at the end of the westbound Central Line platform at Holborn, photographed in July 1993.

Down Street

Dogged by planning difficulties with the local authority regarding the design of its surface building, Down Street station, mid-way between Dover Street (Green Park) and Hyde Park Corner, did not open to passengers until 15 March 1907. Somewhat hidden down a side street off Piccadilly, and too close to Dover Street and Hyde Park corner stations, Down Street never really attracted sufficient passengers to justify its existence. In the early 1930s the northward extension of the Piccadilly Line to Cockfosters provided the justification to withdraw passenger services from Down Street station. The additional frequency of trains following completion of the extension required a reversing siding and stock storage facilities between Hyde Park Corner and Dover Street and the only feasible way of providing this was by truncating the platforms at Down Street, remodelling the station tunnel headwalls and laying the 836-foot siding between the running lines immediately beyond the station. Down Street station was finally closed on 21 May 1932 and the siding came into use a year later on 30 May 1933. The two Otis electric lifts were removed from the station's sixty-foot-deep lift shaft which was subsequently fitted with a large extraction fan to assist ventilation in the tunnels. At the same time nearby Dover Street station was refurbished, the lifts replaced by escalators and the name changed to Green Park.

The disused station did not, however, descend into obscurity. With war approaching, Down Street was drawn to the attention of the Railway Executive Committee as a potential safe haven for its

Below: The graceful entrance to Down Street station, hidden discreetly away in Down Street, adjacent to Down Street Mews.

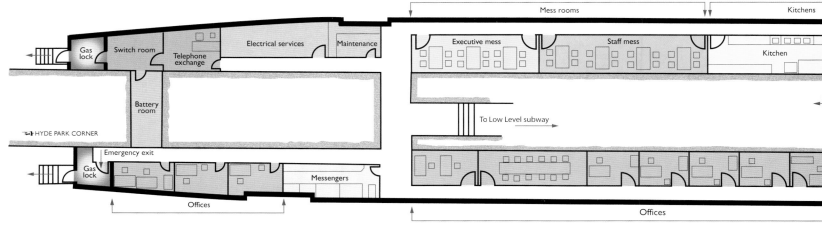

DOWN STREET PLATFORMS

SHOWING LAYOUT OF OFFICES & ACCOMMODATION AS USED DURING SECOND WORLD WAR

Gas locks	Telecoms	Staff accommodation
Offices	Stores, plant, services	Kitchen
Messengers	Executive accommodation	Platforms
		LPTB

headquarters in event of sustained aerial bombing of London. The committee, originally conceived as an advisory body set up by the Ministry of Transport to assist the government in the formulation of rail transport policy, consisted of senior executives of the 'Big Four' railway companies (GWR, LMS, LNER and SR) and the London Passenger Transport Board. At the outbreak of war the railways were taken under government control and the committee became a co-ordinating body between the railway companies and the recently created Ministry of War Transport; the committee chairman, Sir Alan Anderson, also taking on the role of Controller of Railways at the Ministry.

The task of converting Down Street to an emergency headquarters for the Railway Executive Committee was delegated to Gerald Cole-Deacon, the committee secretary, all the necessary structural alterations were put in hand by the London Passenger Transport Board and electrical and communications apparatus installed by the London Midland & Scottish Railway. Construction was still under way when war was declared but thereafter the work was rapidly completed. Below ground, walls were built along the platform edge to segregate the new occupants from the running lines, and behind them a complex of offices, conference rooms, domestic facilities and dormitories was constructed. More offices were created in one of the two subways connecting the lower lift landing to the platforms. An unusual feature of Down Street station was that whilst it was

provided with a conventional emergency escape shaft containing a spiral iron staircase there was also a secondary emergency escape route consisting of a rising flight of steps that terminated at a high-level subway that gave access to the emergency spiral stairway one third of the way up the shaft. This subway was converted into a suite of bathrooms and toilets for the use of senior members of staff. Later in the war a small electric lift was installed in the centre of the stairway shaft.

In the autumn of 1940, during a particularly severe bombing raid, the Down Street headquarters was utilised by Prime Minister Winston Churchill as an emergency conference facility for the War Cabinet. Thereafter, the War Cabinet met there with increasing frequency, using the committee's conference room and executive offices, normally at night during the bombing raids when few Railway Executive staff were on site. Eventually, a small suite of offices dedicated to the use of the War Cabinet was constructed in the disused lift shaft, but by the time construction work was completed the blitz had come to an end and the facility was no longer required. Churchill and his wife continued to use Down Street as alternative sleeping quarters from March 1941 until November 1943 when a more sophisticated reserve cabinet war room and Prime Ministerial accommodation, code-named ANSON, was constructed in the basement of the North Rotunda in Horseferry Road.

Down Street was vacated at the end of the war and much of it remains today relatively untouched except for the suite of offices in the low-level subway which was swept away in the 1970s to improve access during the installation of new signalling equipment.

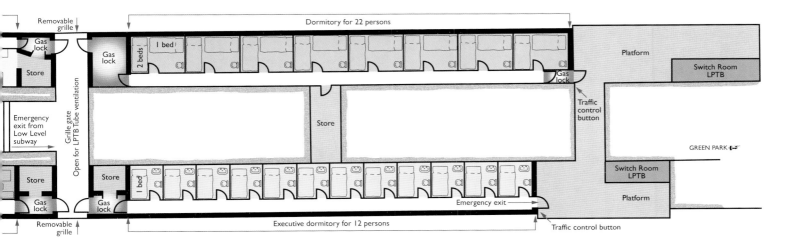

Dormitory for 22 persons

Removable grille

Gas lock

Store

Gas lock

2 beds

1 bed

Emergency exit from Low Level subway

Grille gate
Open for LPTB Tube ventilation

Store

Gas lock

Gas lock

Store

Store

1 bed

Removable grille

Executive dormitory for 12 persons

Emergency exit

Traffic control button

Traffic control button

Platform

Switch Room LPTB

GREEN PARK

Switch Room LPTB

Platform

Right: The narrow staircase down from the surface building at Down Street. Notice on the right the wartime blast door fitted with compression latches to ensure a gas-tight seal and an eye-level observation spy-hole.

Right: A view looking up the alternative emergency exit stairway which has been partitioned to provide additional accommodation.

Below right: The base of the emergency exit shaft, now fitted with a modern, aluminium spiral staircase made necessary because Down Street is designated as an emergency egress route from the Piccadilly Line. The silver-coloured door to the right of the stairway once gave access to a small lift, (removed many years ago), that ran up through the centre of the original spiral stairs. The red door to the far right of the photograph opens into the ventilation fan room located at the bottom of the station's old lift shaft.

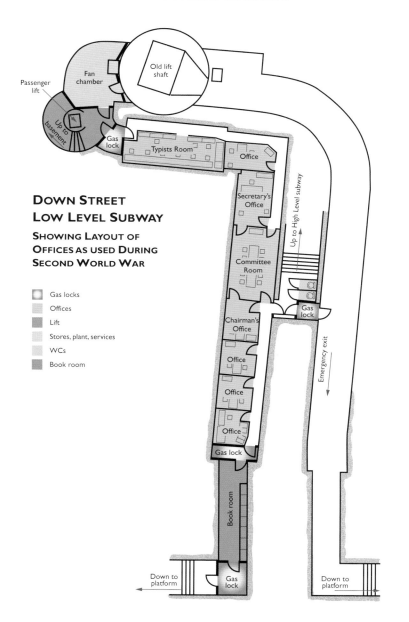

DOWN STREET
LOW LEVEL SUBWAY

SHOWING LAYOUT OF OFFICES AS USED DURING SECOND WORLD WAR

- Gas locks
- Offices
- Lift
- Stores, plant, services
- WCs
- Book room

Above: The east end of the eastbound platform at Down Street. Along the remaining length of the station a wall was constructed along the platform edge to create the shell of the offices built there. This short length of platform was left in order that, in emergency, senior staff working in the wartime offices could travel by train to or from Down Street, alighting or boarding at the station via the driver's cab. The door to the right gives access to an electrical switchroom.

Right: A view across the lower landing of the original passenger lift shaft showing the entrance subway on the far side.

Left: The entrance subway looking back towards the lower lift landing seen in the photograph above. Whilst the exit subway functions as an emergency exit route and is permanently illuminated and kept clean, the entrance subway is unlit and displays many decades' accumulation of dust.

Opposite: The low-level subway today. All traces of the wartime offices were swept away during the 1970s when the area was cleared to improve access to a new signalling relay room. This view is taken from the position of the former committee room looking towards the top of the stairs down to platform level, off to the right beyond the bridge spanning the eastbound track.

Above: The derelict carcass of the Second World War two-position manual telephone switchboard still survives in the telephone exchange at the west end of the eastbound platform. For reasons not readily discernible, the whole room and everything in it has been sprayed with a thick coating of grey paint. When operational this exchange had connections with the public GPO network, with the London Transport telephone system and those of the four mainline railway companies.

Left: The telephone exchange main distribution frame and relay racks located in a room adjacent to the telephone switchboard and similarly coated in grey paint.

Below left: The electrical switchroom at the west end of the eastbound platform, which provided light and power to the west end of the Down Street complex during wartime and also housed the change-over equipment allowing power to be taken from the grid or the station's own emergency generator. In this room even the light bulb has been painted grey!

Below right: A view along the very narrow access corridor on the westbound platform. The rooms on the left are dormitories, the wall to the right is built along the platform edge and separates the control centre from the westbound running line.

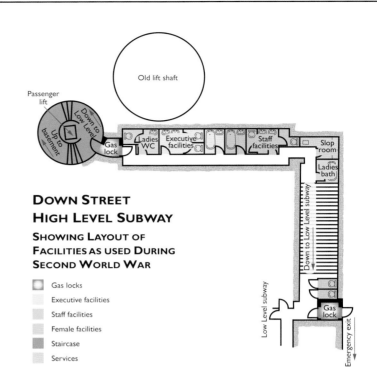

DOWN STREET
HIGH LEVEL SUBWAY

SHOWING LAYOUT OF
FACILITIES AS USED DURING
SECOND WORLD WAR

- Gas locks
- Executive facilities
- Staff facilities
- Female facilities
- Staircase
- Services

Above: The intermediate high-level subway at Down Street was fitted out with ablution facilities. This view shows the gas lock at the point where the subway links to the emergency staircase.

Below left: A bath of wartime vintage still extant in the executive ablutions.
Below: Hand basins and a seemingly rather less-than-private lavatory in the staff toilet facilities.

Above: Modern relay interlocking equipment in the 1970s that necessitated the clearance of the wartime partitions in the low-level subway.

Brompton Road

Construction of the Great Northern, Piccadilly & Brompton Railway started at Knightsbridge in July 1902 and within two years excavation of the two 350-foot-long, twenty-one-foot diameter station tunnels at Brompton Road, the next station up the line, was largely completed. The two sixty-foot-deep lift shafts linking the surface booking hall to the station platforms, along with a smaller diameter emergency exit shaft containing a spiral staircase, were completed in December 1905 after which work on the decorative tiling was started. The station,

Above: The staff entrance to Brompton Road station, located in Cottage Place. The passenger entrance on Brompton Road was demolished in 1972 as part of a road widening scheme.

with its Arts & Crafts style booking hall by the architect Leslie Green, was officially opened by the recently appointed President of the Board of Trade, David Lloyd George, on 15 December 1906.

Due principally to its proximity to the much more conveniently positioned nearby stations at Knightsbridge and South Kensington, Brompton Road did not, from the outset, attract the anticipated number of passengers. To reduce operating costs one of the four passenger lifts (there were two in each vertical shaft) was removed in 1911. The second lift in the same shaft was removed during the late 1920s. Meanwhile it was decided that many trains would not stop at Brompton Road, the familiar warning given by guards as

trains approached the adjacent stations at Knightsbridge and South Kensington – 'Not Stopping At Brompton Road' – being adopted as the title of a long-running West End farce by the playwright Jevan Brandon-Thomas.

Due to manpower shortages at the start of the First World War the booking office was closed and thereafter passengers bought their tickets from the lift attendant. The station closed, supposedly temporarily, in May 1926 at the beginning of the National Strike when underground services were rationalised in order to help conserve the nation's coal supply. At the end of the emergency it was announced that Brompton Road would not re-open but this decision was rescinded in October 1926 in the face of vociferous local opposition. The reprieve did not last long, the closure of Brompton Road being announced towards the end of 1932 as part of a general reorganisation of passenger services in both central London and the suburbs. With the focus of commuter travel now centred upon the rapid transport of passengers from the suburbs to key central locations, rather than shuttling them on short journeys between closely spaced stations within the city, it was decided that a number of lightly patronised stations, including Brompton Road, York Street and Down Street, would be closed in order to reduce journey times. Brompton Road survived, however, until 29 July 1934 while work continued on the improvement of nearby Knightsbridge station where services were briefly curtailed while new escalators were installed.

But Brompton Road station did not slip into immediate obscurity. As early as March 1934 the British Government had begun to make active preparations for the next European war which even then seemed inevitable. Numerous elements of the British establishment, both civil and military, were actively seeking underground accommodation that might offer protection from German bombers which, they had been told, 'would always get through'. The nearby Victoria & Albert Museum had discussed the possibility of using parts of Brompton Road as bomb-proof storage for some of its artefacts but did not begin negotiating terms until after the Munich Crisis in 1938. Unfortunately, and unknown to the V&A, the London Passenger Transport Board (LPTB) which now controlled the London underground system, was already discussing terms with the Commander of the Territorial Army First Anti-Aircraft Division, under the erroneous assumption that joint occupancy would be acceptable. After a somewhat heated exchange it was agreed in November 1938 that the V&A would relinquish its claim

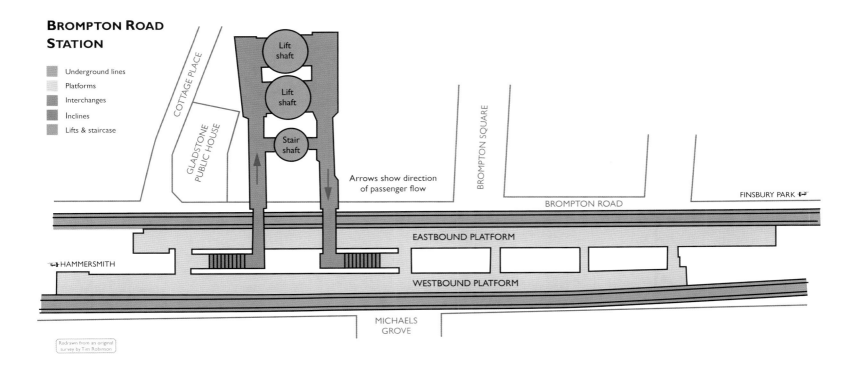

BROMPTON ROAD STATION

- Underground lines
- Platforms
- Interchanges
- Inclines
- Lifts & staircase

COTTAGE PLACE

Lift shaft

Lift shaft

Stair shaft

GLADSTONE PUBLIC HOUSE

Arrows show direction of passenger flow

BROMPTON SQUARE

BROMPTON ROAD

FINSBURY PARK

EASTBOUND PLATFORM

HAMMERSMITH

WESTBOUND PLATFORM

MICHAELS GROVE

Redrawn from an original survey by Tim Robinson

and that the War Office would purchase the westbound platform, lift shafts and surface building for £24,000. Minutes of the agreement record that 'the lift shafts are suitable for the construction of three or more operations rooms and an apparatus room; these rooms can be connected from the spiral staircase. The LPTB is prepared to build the operations and apparatus rooms and to make the ground level bombproof.'

At rail-level, walls were erected to form a barrier along the edge of the westbound platform and rooms constructed within the enclosed space providing accommodation for a teleprinter centre at the east end and welfare facilities at the west end. Intermediate floors were constructed in the lift shaft to provide three circular operations rooms and a communications centre. The upper floor, referred to as Gun Operations Room 1, (GOR 1), housed the central operations room with a raised dais allowing controlling officers a clear view of the plotting tables beneath them and the various status displays mounted on the surrounding wall. Although the Brompton Road Control Centre was a War Office establishment the air defence of London was under the overall control of the headquarters of RAF No.11 Group, Fighter Command, and all information regarding the air situation over the capital was relayed to Brompton Road from the

RAF Group Control Centre at Uxbridge. The next floor down, GOR 2, contained a telephone and telegraph communications centre while the two floors below that, GOR 3 and GOR 4, housed dedicated operations rooms overseeing and controlling anti-aircraft gun-sites to the north and south of London respectively. The final room, situated at platform level, was fitted out as an emergency control room for use if those above were disabled by enemy action.

The Brompton Road Control Centre continued to operate until 1953 when, as part of a radical overhaul of Britain's air defences in the face of the Soviet atomic threat, its function was usurped by three new, heavily protected Anti-Aircraft Operations Rooms on the periphery of London at Lippits Hill, Merstham and Uxbridge. Brompton Road was retained as a reserve operations room until 1956 and parts of the site were used for a while thereafter as offices for the London District Military Command. In 1987 it was proposed as the location of the control bunker for the London Fire and Civil Defence Authority but the scheme was subsequently abandoned. Still owned by the Ministry of Defence, the much altered surface building sees occasional use as the Town Headquarters of the University of London Air Squadron, all the sub-surface areas have been disused for many years.

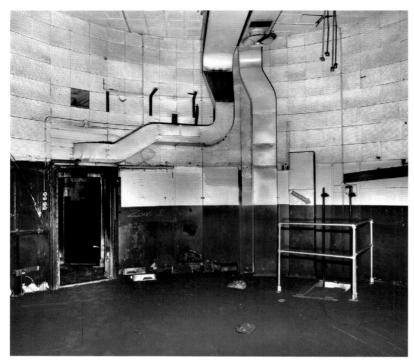

GUN OPERATIONS ROOM No.2

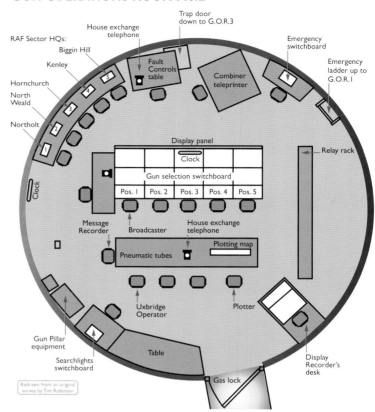

RAF Sector HQs:
Biggin Hill
Kenley
Hornchurch
North Weald
Northolt

House exchange telephone

Trap door down to G.O.R.3

Fault Controls table

Combiner teleprinter

Emergency switchboard

Emergency ladder up to G.O.R.1

Clock

Display panel

Clock

Gun selection switchboard

Pos. 1 | Pos. 2 | Pos. 3 | Pos. 4 | Pos. 5

Relay rack

Message Recorder

Broadcaster

House exchange telephone

Plotting map

Pneumatic tubes

Uxbridge Operator

Plotter

Gun Pillar equipment

Searchlights switchboard

Table

Display Recorder's desk

Gas lock

Redrawn from an original survey by Tim Robinson

Above: Gun Operations Room No.1. In this room the progress of air raids upon London was plotted on a large-scale-map table overlooked by a raised dais manned by the General Officer Commanding and his support staff. Wall mounted lamp units indicated which gun batteries were firing and which were ready for action.

Below: Gun Operations Room No.3. Operators in this room controlled the anti-aircraft gun batteries in the north London area.

Below: Cantilevered from the shaft wall, this steel walkway links the spiral access staircase to Gun Operations Room No.3.

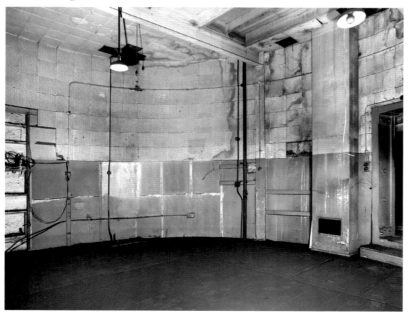

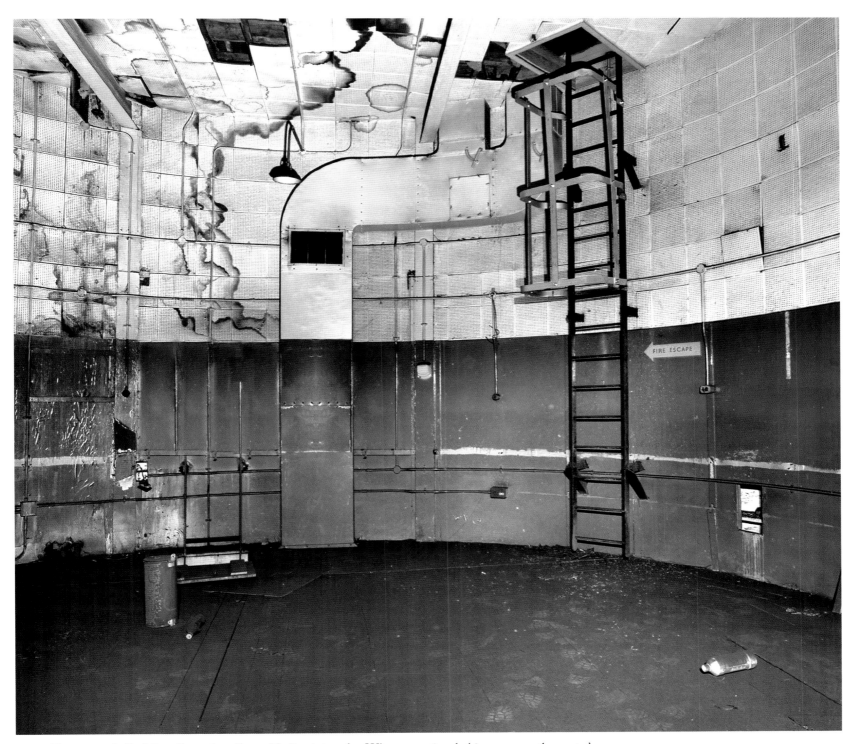

Above: The empty shell of Gun Operations Room No.2 as it is today. When operational, this room was the centre's communication hub *(see plan opposite)*. The steel ladder is an emergency escape route to GOR 1 while the trap door to the left, behind the red fire-blanket container, is the escape route to or from GOR 3.

Above: This photograph vividly illustrates the manner in which the platform at Brompton Road was walled-off from the running lines to provide office accommodation. Here on the westbound side a short length of platform opposite one of the cross passages, just visible in the left foreground, was retained to allow military personnel to disembark from passing trains if required.

Above left: The alighting point for military personnel on the eastbound platform.

Above right: A section of the westbound platform showing the station's characteristic green and brown tiling and one of the three tiled 'Brompton Road' station name panels inset in the tunnel wall.

Left: The eastbound platform at Brompton Road converted into office space for Anti-Aircraft Command. The wall to the right is built along the platform edge. Note the narrowness of the room and the undersides of the two steel bridges carrying the pedestrian subway from the platforms to the lift landing.

Above: The second lift shaft was divided by a mid-feather wall. On one side floors were inserted to provide a series of semi-circular offices. The other side, seen here, was left unobstructed and used for ventilation.
Below: Ventilation plant at the base of the shaft.

Above: A dismantled wartime ventilation fan on the lower lift landing.

Below: Air filters, designed to counter the effects of poison gas, near the entrance to Gun Operations Room No.3.

This page: Three surviving examples of the distinctive almond green and golden brown tiling used at Brompton Road. The lettering is fired into the tiles, not painted on after construction, and must have required careful alignment to produce so neat an appearance. Notice the elegantly stylised portal to the cross passage visible in the photograph top left.

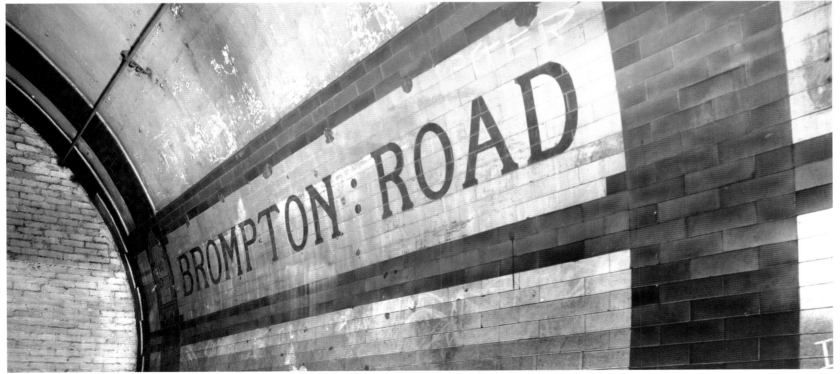

South Kensington

The first lines into South Kensington were laid by the Metropolitan Railway in 1856. The first section of the Metropolitan District Railway (later to be known as the District Line) was opened between Westminster and South Kensington in December 1868. At the same time the Metropolitan Railway was extending its own lines south and west through Notting Hill, Kensington High Street and Brompton to join the Metropolitan District at South Kensington. By the early 1900s the Metropolitan District Railway was extending suburban branches to Ealing, Richmond, Hounslow and Wimbledon and the increase in traffic was causing congestion where the lines headed into the city between South Kensington and Mansion House. As early as 1896 the company had considered the feasibility of relieving congestion by means of a deep-level electrified express route from Earls Court to Mansion House with only one intermediate stop at Charing Cross. Electric traction was still an unproven technology at that time however, and finance difficult to raise, so little progress was made with the express route scheme although it was not immediately dropped in its entirety.

In 1902 the Great Northern, Piccadilly & Brompton Railway (GNP&BR), later to be known as the Piccadilly Line, proposed a deep-level tube line from South Kensington to Piccadilly Circus. In the same year the GNP&BR and the Metropolitan District Railway became part of Yerkes' London Electric Railways Company and under his control an expanded version of the earlier GNP&BR scheme came to fruition with a line running between Finsbury Park and Hammersmith with, amongst others, a station at South Kensington which opened on 8 January 1907. Electrification, pushed ahead by Yerkes, and the inauguration of the GNP&BR, rendered the Metropolitan District express route largely redundant, but not before a certain amount of tunnelling had been completed for its route through South Kensington. A short length of station tunnel was built adjacent to the GNP&BR platform tunnels together with a series of interchange passageways near the lifts and a section of wide-diameter tunnel west of the station where a junction would have been formed between the express line and the GNP&BR. Had the Metropolitan District Railway's deep-level scheme gone ahead then both companies' eastbound trains would have used the same platform with the lines diverging at a junction east of the station. Westbound trains would have used separate platforms with the lines merging at the junction west of the station. To facilitate this, and

in anticipation of the express route being completed, the eastbound GNP&BR station tunnel was positioned above the westbound in order that the westbound GNP&BR line should be on the same level as the westbound Metropolitan District line.

As the express route was never built, the station tunnel and associated passageways were rendered redundant for traffic purposes although a variety of uses were found for them over the decades that followed. During the First World War, for example, the tunnels were used for the safe storage of artefacts from the Victoria & Albert Museum and of ceramics from the Royal Collection. A railway signalling school was established in the disused station tunnel in 1927 and continued in operation until the outbreak of war in 1939 when hydrophonic equipment was installed to give warning of enemy bombs falling in the river Thames. Data from the bomb-monitoring equipment would be used to determine whether the emergency flood-gates in the tube tunnels should be activated. When escalators were installed at South Kensington in the 1970s during the station refurbishment their shafts cut through the abandoned station tunnel. With the lifts taken out of use the old GNP&BR surface building was abandoned, all passengers henceforth using the former Metropolitan District Railway station for access to all lines.

Below: The open top of one of the lift shafts at South Kensington, retained for ventilation purposes.

Above: A view looking down the disused lift shaft seen opposite. The entrances to the lower landing can be seen at the bottom of the shaft.

Above: A view across the base of one of the disused lift shafts with the Piccadilly Line corridor
visible through the ventilation grilles which now secure the lower lift landings.

Above left: Located at the west end of the now demolished Metropolitan District westbound platform, the circular shaft lining segments mark the top of the emergency staircase to the Piccadilly Line platforms below. This was taken out of use when the lifts were replaced by escalators in 1973.

Above right: The bottom of the emergency staircase shaft, to the right, with its entrance blocked by a concrete wall.

Right: The Piccadilly Line lower lift landing, taken out of use in 1973 and now used only for ventilation.

Above: This short length of tunnel is all that remains of the abortive District Line deep-level express-line tunnel, which had been adapted for a number of functions including a First World War repository for art treasures, an inter-war signalling school and a Second World War hydrophonic bomb-monitoring station. Most of what survived was destroyed when the new escalator tunnels were cut through it in the early 1970s.

Charing Cross platforms on the Jubilee Line

Work started in 1971, at a time of economic uncertainty, on the construction of what was then to be called the Fleet Line but which was later renamed the Jubilee Line in honour of Queen Elizabeth's Silver Jubilee in 1977. It was intended that the line should run from Baker Street, through central London towards Lewisham, thus relieving pressure on the Bakerloo Line which was creaking under the weight of passengers using it, but difficulty in finding finance for the scheme led to its implementation in stages. The first stage to be completed was a two-and-a-half-mile section from Baker Street to a terminus at Charing Cross with intermediate stops at Bond Street and Green Park which opened in May 1979. Accommodation of the new Jubilee Line platforms involved the radical reconstruction and integration of the existing underground stations around Charing Cross. The Jubilee Line platforms lie between those of the former Strand station on the Northern Line and Trafalgar Square station on the Bakerloo Line, and to facilitate the building and tunnelling work Strand station was temporarily closed on 4 June 1973. During the reconstruction, a long-required underground passenger interchange tunnel was provided to join the Northern and Bakerloo Line platforms.

At the time of the station's opening it was expected that Charing Cross would be only the temporary terminus of the Jubilee Line and plans had already been prepared for its eastward continuation towards Lewisham and, indeed, the running tunnels already extended some distance beyond Charing Cross towards Aldwych which was expected to be the next stop on the line. The demographic changes brought about by the regeneration of the London Docklands, however, brought about a radical change in transport policy. A new route was proposed for the Jubilee Line beyond Green Park encompassing a new interchange at Westminster and an eastward extension via Waterloo, London Bridge and Greenwich, terminating at Stratford. For both technical and traffic reasons it was decided that the new route would progress not from Charing Cross, as first envisaged, but instead from a point just to the south of Green Park. When the first section of the extension was completed from Green Park to Waterloo station in November 1999 the route into Charing Cross, which by now had been relegated to a short branch, was closed to passenger traffic. Soon afterwards the five escalators down to the now disused Jubilee Line platforms at Charing Cross were shut down and access to them closed off.

Since 1999 the section of line between Green Park and Charing Cross has been used by Transport for London only for train reversals. The station and platforms, however, are maintained in good order and are used extensively by film and television companies who require a modern-era London Underground location shoot. Media companies requiring a more period setting utilise the disused tunnels at Aldwych station which are maintained for a similar purpose.

Below: This route diagram on the disused concourse shows Charing Cross as the terminus of the Jubilee Line.

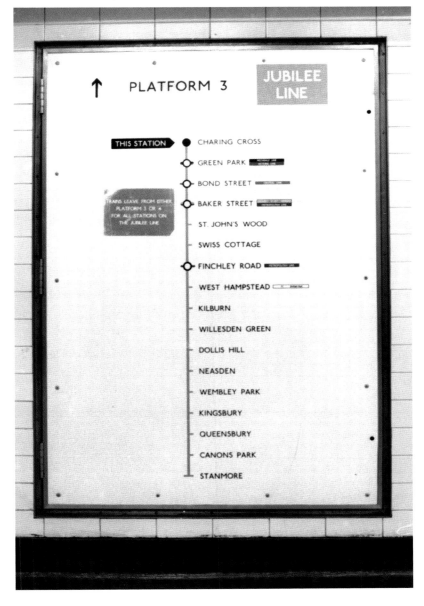

Above: In July 2008 a Jubilee Line train waits at the southbound platform 3 at
Charing Cross waiting to run into the reversing siding.

Above: The now disused and abandoned escalators up to the Bakerloo Line from the Jubilee Line concourse at Charing Cross.

Left: Jubilee Line route map on the concourse at Charing Cross. A train can be seen standing at northbound platform 4 through the cross passage. To the far right is the bottom of the flight of escalators leading up to the Northern Line.

Above: Disused escalators that once carried passengers from the Jubilee Line concourse up to the Northern Line at Charing Cross.

Left: Northbound platform 4, showing the distinctive form of station signage used on the Jubilee Line.

Below left: Deep below Trafalgar Square a works tunnel headed away from the Jubilee Line station to a point adjacent to the Sainsbury Wing of the National Gallery. A narrow gauge railway was laid in the tunnel and used for the evacuation of spoil from the excavation. The passageway, seen here, is now blocked by a concrete plug. Piles of ceiling lining panels for the Jubilee Line platforms are piled in front of the block wall.

Below right: A works tunnel, never intended for passenger use, excavated to give easy access to the site during construction of the Jubilee Line.

Chapter 3

DEEP-LEVEL SHELTERS

From the first year of its existence in 1933 the London Passenger Transport Board (LPTB) had been looking at schemes to increase the capacity on its most congested lines, particularly the section of the Northern Line between Morden and Edgware Road. A number of proposals were put forward throughout the late 1930s, including the construction of relief lines between Balham and Kennington and between Waterloo and Camden Town, but none had been implemented at the outbreak of war in September 1939. Meanwhile, following the accession to power of Hitler as Chancellor of Germany in 1934, the threat of war had been in the air and active measures were under way, from 1935, to provide the citizens of London with some measure of protection against air raids, under the aegis of the recently created Ministry of Home Security. These two seemingly unrelated threads were brought together as a consequence of the start of the German aerial assault against London in October 1940.

Following a protracted series of meetings between Lord Ashfield, chairman of the LPTB, and Herbert Morrison, the Minister for Home Defence, it was agreed that a system of deep underground shelters would be constructed on alignments beneath existing LPTB tube stations on the Northern and Central Lines, and that at the cessation of hostilities the LPTB would be given the option of purchasing these with the object of incorporating them in new express tube routes running parallel with the existing lines. The agreement appears to have been a very loose one; there was no compulsion upon the LPTB to purchase the tunnels at a later date.

Above: The north entrance to Clapham Common deep-level shelter, located on Clapham High Street near its junction with Carpenters Place. The original circular entrance 'pillbox' is largely obscured by the more recent brick-built extensions seen to the right of this photograph.
Below: Clapham Common shelter south entrance, located at the junction of Clapham High Street and Clapham Park Road, London SW4.

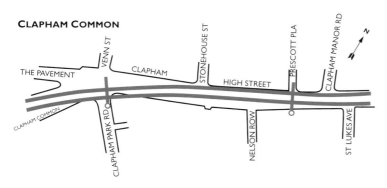

Above: The east entrance to the Goodge Street shelter in Chenies Street at its junction with North Crescent, London WC1. Now used as a secure storage facility, it is known as the Eisenhower Centre, a reference to its wartime use as an American military headquarters and communications centre.

Right: The west entrance to the Goodge Street shelter adjacent to Whitfield Memorial Church on Tottenham Court Road.

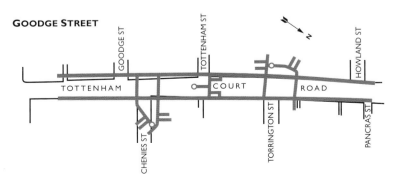

GOODGE STREET

Meanwhile the government gained access to LPTB tunnelling and engineering expertise, while the distant prospect of recouping the cost from the Board in the post-war years to some extent justified the great expense of the project.

Initially, after a few false starts, ten sites were chosen at Clapham South, Clapham Common, Clapham North, Stockwell, Oval, Goodge Street, Camden Town, Belsize Park, Chancery Lane and St. Paul's. The St. Paul's scheme was abandoned following objections from the Cathedral authorities who feared that the tunnelling might endanger the foundations of the building; the proposed Oval shelter was also abandoned after work had progressed some way when difficult, water-bearing ground was encountered. It was estimated in November 1940 that construction of the shelters would cost £15,000,000 (although the final bill was more than double that), and that if work began immediately they could be completed by the summer of the following year. The design of the shelters has led to a certain degree of confusion amongst historians in recent years. Each shelter consists of two parallel tubes 400 yards (366 metres) in length of standard LPTB design lined with bolted cast-iron segments. However, whereas the running tunnels of the tube railway system are thirteen-feet six-inches in diameter, the shelter tunnels are sixteen-feet six inches, which has led some observers to erroneously assume that the intention was that they should become stations on the proposed post-war high-speed line. In fact, the records of the planning meetings indicate that the shelters were to be constructed beneath those stations that the express trains would not stop at and that the larger diameter tube was insisted upon by the Ministry of Home Security. The increased size was to allow the shelters to be constructed with an intermediate floor yet still maintain sufficient headroom for shelterers on each level.

It was originally expected that each shelter would accommodate 9,600 people but subsequent improvements to both welfare facilities

and overall standards of accommodation reduced this figure to 8,000. Access was made via two vertical shafts positioned towards each end of the shelter and topped by monolithic circular bomb-proof block houses fitted with blast doors and gas seals. The shafts were fitted with double-spiral stairs, rather like the double-helix DNA molecule, designed to give independent access to each floor of the shelter from a common entrance. The centre of each spiral provided space for a small electric lift, which was used only to transport provisions for the underground canteens and tea bars. Alternative entrances were provided via stairways leading down from the platforms of the tube stations above, but the LPTB objected to these being used. Completion of the shelters was delayed by a number of factors

Above: The north entrance rotunda to Stockwell deep-level shelter, located on an island site at the corner of South Lambeth Road and Clapham Road, London SW9. The mural decoration is by Brian Barnes, well known for his similar large-scale works in Brixton, Stockwell and elsewhere. Barnes was a founder member of the Battersea Power Station Community Group whose aim is the preservation of the threatened deco-period structure.

including shortages of suitable labour and difficulties encountered in the supply of the 24,000 tons of tunnel lining segments. All were sufficiently complete to be handed over by the contractors to the shelter management committee in November 1942.

Sometime earlier, in mid-1941, the government indicated that it was having second thoughts about completing the deep-level shelters, partly because the Select Committee on National Expenditure had questioned the steeply rising costs but principally because of the fear of engendering a 'shelter mentality' amongst the population of the capital. The more pessimistic members of the government had feared

STOCKWELL STATION

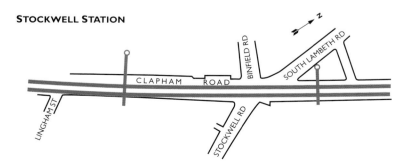

Above: The south entrance to the Stockwell shelter strikes a somewhat surreal pose amongst the flats and lock-up garages in Studley Road, SW4.

since the inception of the Air Raid Precautions organisation in 1924 that on the first sounding of the air-raid siren the working population of London would dive into the shelters and refuse to leave until the war was over, much to the detriment of war production and industrial output. Ultimately three of the deep-level shelters were never opened to the public and the Ministry of Home Defence resisted pressure to open the others to the public until more-or-less compelled to do so by the arrival of the Flying Bomb and later the V2 missiles during the latter half of 1944. Clapham North, Clapham South, Stockwell, Camden Town, and Belsize Park opened their doors to the public in July 1944 but the take-up was only modest. At most, only 12,297 of the 40,000 available places were occupied. Belsize Park and Clapham North were closed in October 1944, the others in the early days of the following May.

Alternative uses were found for several of the deep-level shelters both during the Second World War and in the immediate post-war years. Clapham Common, for example, was used briefly as a hostel for American troops in 1943 and was reserved in the following year as emergency sleeping accommodation for War Office and other government department employees. From July 1945 until 1951 it was used as a document store by the Admiralty and the Probate Record Office. In February 1944 the shelter was fitted with communications equipment enabling it to function, albeit only briefly, as an emergency backup to the facilities established earlier in the tunnels at Chancery Lane, described below. Clapham South was utilised as a weekend troop billet and leave hostel throughout 1945 and in 1948 rose to prominence as a temporary hostel for the first group of Jamaican immigrants who arrived in Britain aboard the *Empire Windrush*. Three years later, in 1951, it was used as an inexpensive hotel for young visitors to the Festival of Britain, the following year it housed troops stationed in London for the funeral of King George VI and was again used as a hotel during the Coronation celebrations of Queen Elizabeth II. The Stockwell shelter was used variously and briefly during 1945 as a hostel for British and American troops. Between 1947 and 1951 it was used as a temporary archive store by the Public Records Office and several other government departments and London museums. Similarly, Camden Town, which had already seen service in the autumn of 1943 as a hostel for British and Dominion troops, was used as a service hostel between 1945 and 1947 and thereafter, until 1952, as a storage facility for various government departments. Belsize Park remained unused for a year after its closure in October 1944 but was then used until June 1951 as a document

repository by the Board of Trade, Ministry of Health, the National Debt Office and the War Office.

Goodge Street played a more pivotal role in the later years of the war. In March 1943 work was nearing completion on the conversion of half of the underground shelter into a communications centre for base command of the European Theatre of Operations United States Army (ETOUSA). Facilities provided in the centre included an Army and Navy message centre, an emergency telephone switchboard, radio terminals and a British Government code-room. Meanwhile, the remaining section became an emergency standby signals centre for the Chief of Staff to Supreme Allied Commander (COSSAC) during the initial preparations for the invasion of Europe. Facilities here replicated those already established in a bomb-proof basement some forty feet beneath Selfridges department store which included a 104-position telephone switchboard and the SIGSALY encryption apparatus, consisting of forty racks of electronic equipment weighing in excess of fifty tons, used to encode high-level communications between the British and American governments, including personal messages between Winston Churchill and President Roosevelt.

Following the departure of the Americans at the end of the war Goodge Street too was utilised as a temporary store for government documents until 1951 when it was refitted to serve as the London District Assembly Centre. On 21 May 1956 a serious fire destroyed much of the accommodation there although the structure of the tunnel itself suffered surprisingly little damage. In more recent years the Goodge Street tunnels have been occupied by a commercial high-security storage company.

From January 1944 a section of the Chancery Lane shelter was used as a hostel for servicewomen but was transferred for a short time in 1945 to the Public Records Office whose peacetime offices, prior to the move to new facilities at Kew, were in Chancery Lane. The shelter was also home to a shadowy organisation known only as the Inter-Services Research Bureau, which was in fact a top-secret research and development arm of the Special Operations Executive, an organisation created in 1940 to conduct espionage, sabotage and reconnaissance in occupied Europe against the Axis powers, and to aid local resistance movements. Towards the end of the war the tunnels also provided accommodation for the reserve war room of the London Civil Defence Region. In July 1952 the Chancery Lane site was transferred to the General Post Office and was extended and adapted to become the home of the *Kingsway* telephone exchange, the detailed history of which is recounted later in this chapter.

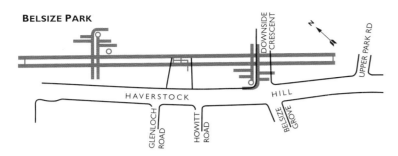

Belsize Park

Each of the deep-level shelters consisted essentially of two parallel tunnels divided horizontally to provide two floors, each separated into four sections which were given distinctive names enabling shelterers quickly to locate their allocated bunks. At Belsize Park the sections were given the names of famous explorers and adventurers; those in the northern tunnel, which was the only tunnel actually used as a civilian shelter, the areas were named Godley, Baden-Powell, Frobisher, Ashurst, Scott, Livingstone, Rhodes and Kimberley. Those in the south tunnel, which was retained for government use and never opened to the public, were named Cook, Hudson, Dampier, Jameson, Milner, Vancouver, Phillip and Wolfe.

The northern tunnel of the Belsize Park shelter was first opened to the public on 23 July 1944 but was never heavily patronised and closed on 21 October of the same year, the few regular occupants being transferred to Camden Town. During the immediate post-war years Belsize Park, like several of the other deep-level shelters, was used for the storage of government documents. In more recent years it has been leased by a commercial security storage company and is used as a high-security data storage facility.

Above: The southern entrance to the Belsize Park shelter at the junction of Downside Crescent and Haverstock Hill.

Below left: An isometric drawing of a deep-level shelter showing the arrangement of the access shafts and the relationship of the shelter tunnels with the existing tube tunnels.

Below right: The top landing of the small service lift shaft in the northern entrance building. The handrail of the upper level spiral staircase is just visible to the left of the lift.

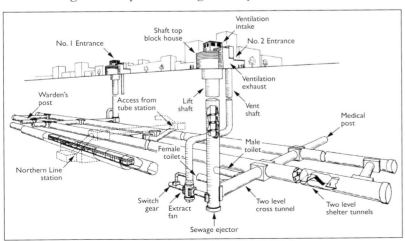

Above: Wartime bunks still in situ in the upper level of the northern shelter tunnel.

Above: A view across the connecting corridor joining the two shelter tunnels.
Below: Located in a side chamber near the base of the northern entrance shaft, this large extraction fan vents vitiated air to the surface via a vertical shaft that emerges in a compound close to the surface entrance building.

Above: The bottom of one of the vertical ventilation shafts showing the air passage in the background.
Below: The switchroom adjacent to the fan chamber, with a mercury arc rectifier glowing a rather eerie blue behind.

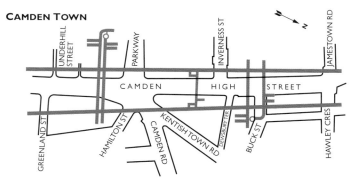

CAMDEN TOWN

Camden Town

The various sections of the Camden Town shelter were given the names of military generals in alphabetical order: Allenby, Bruce, Clive, Dalhousie, French, Gordon, Haigh, Kitchener, Lawrence, Marlborough, Napier, Outram, Plumer, Roberts, Townshend and Wellington. The shelter opened to the public on 16 July 1944, although it had been in use as a hostel for some 2,000 British and Dominion troops since September 1943. It finally closed on 7 May 1945. For a few years after the war the tunnels were used as a military leave hostel and a repository for government documents. During the 1970s they were used as sets for the television programmes *Doctor Who* and *Blake's Seven*, and more recently they have been occupied by a secure document storage company.

Above: The south entrance adjacent to Underhill Street. The north entrance in Buck Street is now used only as an emergency exit by the current occupants.
Below left: The northern extremity of section 'T' (for Townshend).
Below right: A view inside the main entrance building showing the service lift and stairway.

Above: Original bunks still in position on the lower floor of the east tunnel at Camden Town. On the left are three tiers of bunks running the length of the tunnel; a single at ground level, a double at mid-height and another single near the ceiling. The central double bunk can be folded up to increase the clearance in the walkway when not in use. On the right the bunks are arranged transversely in stacks of three with each pair of stacks divided by a partial partition into separate bays.

Above: The upper floor of the west tunnel adapted as a commercial document store. All the original bunks and partitions have been stripped out and modern Dexion racking installed.

Opposite: The lower floor of the west tunnel. Here the existing bunks have been pressed into use as shelving.

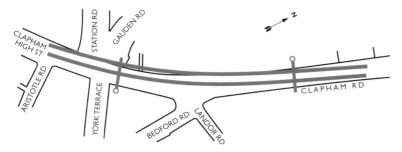

CLAPHAM NORTH

Clapham North

The north entrance to the Clapham North shelter stands adjacent to Russell Pickering House on the west side of Clapham Road, SW4. The south entrance is in a compound behind Clapham North station between Bedford Road and Clapham High Street. The shelter was opened on 13 July 1944 but closed a few months later on 21 October due to poor patronage. The few regular shelterers were transferred to Clapham South. Post-war it saw brief use as a government document store and in 1953 was used as a naval billet during the Coronation celebrations.

Above right: The upper floor lift landing. A lift was never installed in this shaft.
Below left: A stairway leading up from the shelter tunnels to the platforms of Clapham North tube station.
Below right: A partially dismantled fan near the west ventilation shaft.

Above: The upper floor of one of the Clapham North shelter tunnels devoid of bunks and other fixtures and fittings. A stairway to the lower floor can be seen in the right foreground.

Above: The lower floor of the west tunnel at Clapham North.

Clapham South

Clapham South shelter was opened to the public on 19 July 1944. The south entrance and tunnel closed on 21 October 1944 but the north tunnel remained in use until 7 May 1945. The shelter was leased to a high-security storage company in 1977 but the lease was terminated in the mid-2000s and the tunnels are now empty. In January 2011 planning permission was granted for the construction of an eight-storey residential block on the surface land associated with the south entrance which, being a listed building, had to be retained and integrated within the new structure, which was completed in 2012.

Above: The south entrance in 2008, with the single-storey administrative offices for the entire deep-level shelter system still in situ to the left of the ventilation shaft

Below: The south entrance, located on the west side of Balham Hill, seen here in 2012 with the circular blockhouse straddled by the new eight-storey residential development.

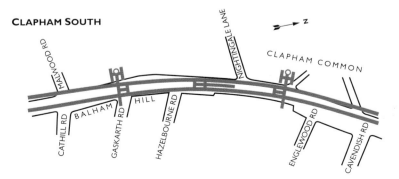

CLAPHAM SOUTH

This page: At Clapham South most of the wartime direction signs have survived in place and in very good condition.

Above: One of the two main switchrooms at Clapham South showing both the wartime electrical equipment and more modern switchgear installed by the storage company that leased the tunnels since 1977. The cabinets to the right are wartime star-delta starters for the ventilation fans, with a mercury arc rectifier in the background. To the left of the rectifier is a transformer behind which is a red carbon dioxide fire extinguisher unit. To the left, above the bus-bar chamber are a number of lighting distribution switches and below is a group of more modern isolators.

Above right & left: Two views of the lower deck of the Clapham South shelter in use, taken in July 1944. Although not occupied to capacity (there are a few vacant bunks visible), the claustrophobic atmosphere of the tube shelters is quite evident.

Right: This photograph of the north entrance building was probably taken in July 1944, shortly before it was brought into use, or possibly a little earlier as the fencing around the compound is still unfinished. The prominent ventilation ducts on the tops of the buildings, and the tall timber and corrugated steel ventilation towers close by, were regarded as eyesores when they were first constructed and were quickly removed at the end of the war. At those locations where new uses were found for the shelter tunnels smaller and less conspicuous inlet and outlet ventilation ducts were constructed. In the right background of this photograph can be seen some of the spoil resulting from the excavation of the tunnels, heaped up on Clapham Common.

Chancery Lane

In the 1950s it was thought that if Britain was to survive a nuclear war, a resilient communications system was essential to ensure the continuity of government. At that time such resilience was offered in part by the buried, long-distance trunk cables that formed the core of the GPO telephone system. Whilst these cables were relatively immune from disruption on their cross-country routes they were dangerously exposed where they emerged at their terminal points, usually telephone exchanges in the centres of the larger cities, which were prime Soviet targets.

To counter this threat a series of underground telephone exchanges were built in tunnels deep below the centres of London, Birmingham and Manchester, the three cities regarded as most at risk. Each was allocated a code name of

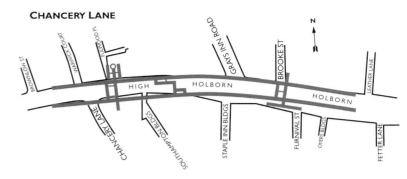

significance to its location; the London exchange was known as *Kingsway*, Manchester's as *Guardian* (after the city's long established newspaper), and Birmingham's as *Anchor* (the silver mark used by the city's proof house).

The Chancery Lane shelter was selected as the location for *Kingsway* in 1949 and by 1952 installation of the telecommunications equipment was under way, extensions to the south of the original tunnels having already been completed. Within ten years, however, the introduction of Subscriber Trunk Dialling (STD) together with the development of the decentralised sector switching scheme for London, led to a decline in the importance of *Kingsway*. In 1979 it was announced that *Kingsway* would close within a year although parts of the tunnels were used for some years afterwards to house various British Telecom computer systems. Briefly, too, *Kingsway* was a temporary home to the British Government's emergency operations centre, known as *Pindar*, while the permanent site was under construction beneath the MoD headquarters in Whitehall.

Left: The discreet pedestrian entrance to the *Kingsway* exchange, via the frontage of the long-disused Chancery Lane tube station at 31-33 High Holborn.

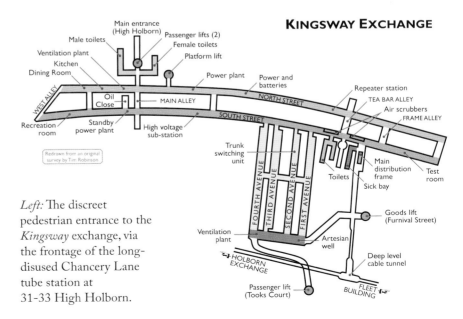

Above left: The goods entrance to *Kingsway* in Furnival Street, showing the lifting gantry above the door. A 9 cwt lift was fitted in the Furnival Street shaft and while this was sufficient for transporting the necessary telecoms plant underground it could not handle the four diesel generator sets required for the exchange's power station. After protracted negotiations with London Transport it was agreed that these should be brought to Chancery Lane station by train from Lillie Bridge maintenance yard and lowered into shelter tunnels via a ten-ton platform lift.

Above right: Spiral staircase from 'Tea Bar Alley' to the upper floor of the exchange.

Below left: The bronze-coloured door to the far left of this photograph is the bottom of the 100-feet deep passenger lift shaft from the High Holborn entrance, with door to the emergency staircase to its right. The red blast door is the main entrance into the telephone exchange tunnels.

Opposite Above: The recreation room and bar with its distinctive 1970s colour scheme.

Opposite left: The dining room, also still retaining its 1970s décor. The size of this room gives some indication of the number of people who worked in the exchange at its busiest period.

Opposite right: The kitchen adjacent to the main dining room, with serving hatches visible in the left-hand wall.

Above: Under emergency conditions the full 1.5 Megawatt load of the *Kingsway* exchange could be met by its own underground power station which contained four 500 kVA Ruston Hornsby alternator sets, two of which can be seen in this photograph.

Opposite: Low-tension (440 volt and 240 volt) switchgear in the exchange substation. The circuit breaker labelled 'LFB Air Plant Shut Down Switch' is provided so that, in event of a fire underground, the London Fire Brigade can immediately shut down the exchange ventilation fans.

Above: The Main Distribution Frame. All incoming and outgoing cables serving *Kingsway* terminate on this frame and are jumpered from here to the relevant exchange apparatus.

Above: A view along Third Avenue, one of the series of new tunnels excavated by the GPO south of the original shelter tunnels. Once crowded with telecommunications equipment it is now just an empty shell.

Below left: Auxiliary plant at the junction of South Street and Main Alley, with the end of a standby generator set just visible in the distance.

Below right: The top of a staircase leading to a cross passage linking the two main tunnels.

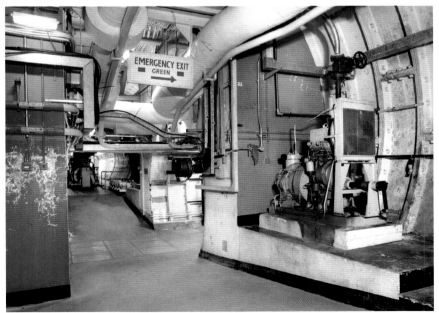

Chapter 4

THE SURREY DEEP-LEVEL SHELTERS

At the start of the Second World War it was expected that the main German assault would take the form of sustained daylight-bombing raids. Very soon, however, it became apparent that Britain's air defences were too strong for daylight bombing to be effective and night-time raids, particularly on moonlit nights, became the norm. Frightened from their beds, thousands of Londoners sought refuge on the edges of the city and to cope with this nightly self-evacuation, Surrey County Council constructed a series of large, deep-level shelters in the chalk downs of what where then the still sparsely populated suburbs of the east Surrey.

Five shelters, each capable of accommodating between five and six thousand shelterers, were planned for Ashley Road, Epsom; Longdown Lane, Epsom; Brighton Road, Coulsdon; Godstone Road, Kenley and a location in the Chipstead Valley. The latter site was abandoned when ground conditions were found to be unsuitable. Their layout and relative remoteness indicates that they were designed for shelterers travelling from some distance, rather than local residents urgently responding to an air-raid siren. All were built to a similar basic design although adapted to local conditions, with three parallel main passageways approximately seventy-five metres long intersected by six lateral passages each sixty-two metres in length. The Coulsdon shelter was an exception to this design having only two lateral passages.

A little further to the east the vast network of tunnels and chambers that comprised Chislehurst Caves – the former chalk mine, tourist attraction and First World War explosives storage depot – was pressed into service as an air-raid shelter for over 15,000 night-time evacuees.

Longdown Lane, Epsom

The entrance to the Epsom Down shelter is in a small wood on the edge of Epsom golf course. Shortly after the war the cutting leading up to the entrance was infilled with domestic rubbish and all trace of the shelter's existence obliterated, although its location and layout are recorded in documents held in the Surrey County archives. Recently the author, with the assistance of other members of the underground exploration group *Subterranea Britannica*, attempted to dig out the entrance.

Below: With the permission of the golf club a mini-digger was brought on site and excavations made to a depth of some fifteen feet. It was clear that the digging was in the right location because quantities of domestic refuse, including old washing machines, were being brought to the surface. Unfortunately, time ran out and the search was suspended without conclusion.

Brighton Road, Coulsdon

With only two lateral passages, the Coulsdon shelter is somewhat smaller than the others tunnelled under the North Downs. In 1949 the vacant tunnels were acquired by the firm of Cox, Hargreaves & Thomson Ltd, who were specialist manufacturers of high precision optical components. They required premises that were vibration-free and with stable year-round atmospheric conditions, and the shelter tunnels offered ideal conditions. A few minor alterations to the arrangement of the tunnel entrances were made at that time. In 1961 a boardroom disagreement about the future direction of the company resulted in two of the directors leaving the company and setting up their own business, Optical Surfaces Ltd, in the somewhat larger air-raid shelter at Kenley. Cox, Hargreaves & Thomson was wound-up in 1978 although production at Coulsdon had ceased several years previously. Shortly afterwards the tunnels were used by a car repair business but by the 1980s were used for little more than fly-tipping, which quickly resulted in the three entrances being blocked by having mounds of earth bulldozed into them.

Below: The blocked main entrance tunnel, looking towards the Brighton Road.

Right: Schematic layout diagram of the Coulsdon shelter showing the structure as-built, superimposed upon the design originally proposed.

Below: After the main entrance to the shelter was blocked in the 1990s, a hole was cut through the roof of the central entrance dog-leg to gain access. This remained open for many years but was eventually blocked during construction of the Coulsdon bypass.

COULSDON AIR-RAID SHELTER

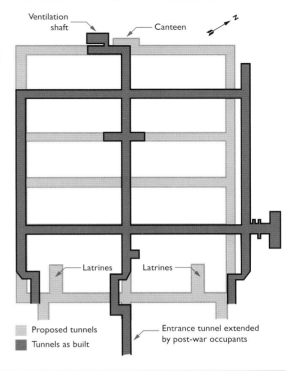

Ventilation shaft

Canteen

Latrines

Latrines

Proposed tunnels

Tunnels as built

Entrance tunnel extended by post-war occupants

Opposite: The middle longitudinal tunnel. This was cleared by Cox, Hargreaves & Thompson in order to provide a very long chamber in which to test the focus of the lenses manufactured at Coulsdon.

Right: The southern lateral tunnel, used as a motor repair workshop after Cox, Hargreaves & Thompson moved out in 1978.

Below left: The piece of equipment abandoned in the bay in the centre of this photograph is a polishing machine, left behind by Cox, Hargreaves & Thompson, capable of polishing mirrors up to eighty-inches in diameter.

Below right: This appears to be an unfinished length of passageway where, perhaps, work was suspended when the original design for the shelter was abandoned.

Kenley

For a few years after the Second World War the Kenley shelter, located on the east side of Godstone Road approximately 100 yards from Kenley railway station, was used by Charles Gardener, the owner of Chislehurst Caves, as an underground mushroom farm, but with little success. A few years after the enterprise began the crop was infected by a devastating and ineradicable fungal disease, similar to that which caused such havoc in the Wiltshire quarries which had been adapted for mushroom cultivation, and the business foundered. In 1961 the disused tunnels were acquired by Optical Surfaces Ltd, a spin-off firm from the older company of Cox, Hargreaves & Thomson who occupied the Coulsdon shelter for some years, and used for the manufacture of high-precision optical components.

Above: The main entrance to the Kenley shelter.
Below: Wartime toilet cubicles in the first lateral passage, near the main entrance.

KENLEY AIR-RAID SHELTER

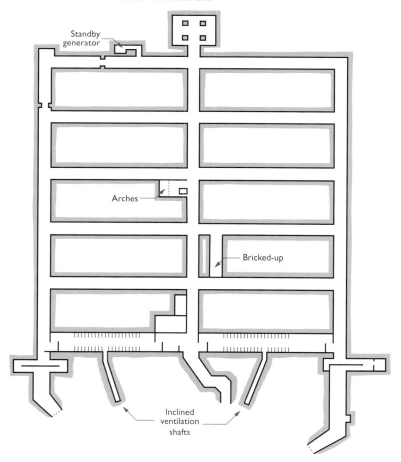

Above: The middle longitudinal passage in the Kenley shelter, now brightly lit and functioning as the central access corridor to the offices and workshops of Optical Surfaces Ltd.

Ashley Road

After decades of abandonment the shelter at Ashley Road, Epsom has in recent years been occupied by an airsoft gaming group.

ASHLEY ROAD AIR-RAID SHELTER

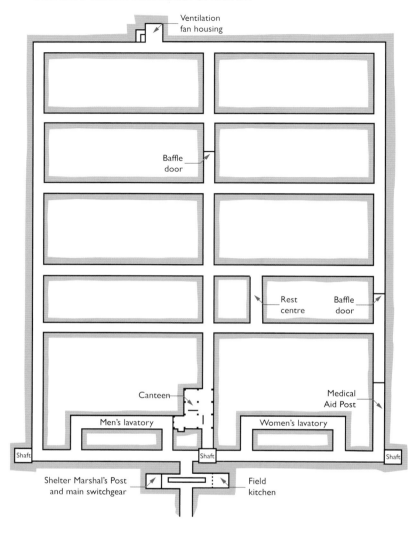

Above left: The somewhat overgrown entrance to the deep-level air-raid shelter at Ashley Road, Epsom.

Left: The left-hand longitudinal tunnel, as seen on the plan above. Notice the various methods used to secure the roof. In the foreground wire mesh has been attached to light steel supports to catch any small fragments of roof that might become detached. Further on, and in the lateral passage to the right, conventional mining arches supporting heavy, corrugated steel panels, have been employed. Elsewhere in the shelter some areas have been left with the roof in a natural state while others are supported by vaulted brick arches.

Opposite: Not shown on the plan, this is the dog-legged passage leading from the entrance to the Shelter Marshal's Post, where the shelter proper begins.

Above: A urinal in the men's toilet, rendered waterproof with by a thick layer of black bitumen.
Below: Intersecting brick arches at the bottom of one of the shelter's two ventilation shafts. The closely-jointed iron pipe appears to be a sewer breather.

Above: A rather claustrophobic group of toilet cubicles.

Below: The remains of the kitchen, canteen and server. Customers would have queued behind the steel railings while waiting to be served.

Chislehurst Caves

Chalk had been mined from underground workings at Chislehurst for centuries, but by the 1830s industrial developments elsewhere led to a sharp decline in demand and quarrying soon ceased thereafter. During the Edwardian period Chislehurst Caves underwent something of a resurgence with their transformation into a popular tourist attraction, but this lucrative activity was brought to a halt by the First World War. On 27 October 1914 the tunnels were requisitioned by the Ministry of Munitions as a storage site for raw materials required for the manufacture of high explosives at Woolwich Arsenal, where the existing storage facilities were becoming increasingly congested. Deliveries began on 10 December 1914 and within weeks the front part of the reputed twenty-two miles of passages and chambers, which had been sealed from the rest of the workings by concrete block walls, were stacked with not only raw materials but in excess of 1,000 tons of processed TNT waiting to be filled into artillery shells at Woolwich.

The caves were finally released by the Ministry of Munitions in July 1920 but do not appear to have been reopened to the public, and by the 1930s they were used by the North Kent Mushroom Company for growing mushrooms. Cultivation of mushrooms at Chislehurst continued until the eve of the Second World War. In 1939 the underground complex was once again requisitioned by the government, this time for use as a public air-raid shelter. Subsequently, bunks, ablutions and extensive welfare facilities were installed for a population of 15,000 south London night-time evacuees. The shelter was closed immediately after VE day and, after a short period of disuse, was reopened to the public as a tourist attraction, a use that has continued to the present day.

Below: The main entrance to Chislehurst Caves, now open as a tourist attraction.

Opposite: A wartime brick boundary wall, adorned by a now badly worn map of the tunnel complex.

Above: The underground chapel in the Chislehurst shelter.

Above: Entrance to the women's lavatory. The notice reading 'No Entry For Men' appears to be stating the obvious.

Below left: Cubicles for chemical closets. Now without 'Elsans' or doors, it is to be hoped that both were adequately provided in wartime.

Below right: The entrance to the gentlemen's lavatory, with no corresponding admonition barring the entrance of women!

Above: Substantial brick and concrete reinforcements have been employed in this area of the caves which forms part of the air-raid shelter.

Chapter 5

SMALLER AIR-RAID SHELTERS

As well as the relatively small number of high-capacity deep-level shelters, a huge array of smaller surface, semi-underground and underground air-raid shelters were built in the London area during the Second World War, either by the various local authorities, large business concerns or as private individual or group initiatives. Many of these have survived and are documented while others, no doubt, still await discovery. A few representative examples of these smaller shelters are described and illustrated in the pages that follow.

Blackheath Hill Tunnel

Below: Blackheath Hill Station circa 1925, shortly after the line fell into disuse. The tunnel is immediately behind the station building.

Above: During demolition of the station building in July 1987 the south portal of the tunnel was fully exposed. It is clear that after its conversion to commercial use the floor level in the tunnel was raised well above track level.

Blackheath Hill tunnel once carried the Greenwich Park branch of the London, Chatham and Dover Railway beneath the Blackheath Hill Road in Greenwich. The branch line, running from Nunhead on the Crystal Palace line to Croomes Hill on the west side of Greenwich Park, was authorised in 1863 but raising capital for its construction proved difficult and work did not begin for several years. The line was opened to Blackheath Hill on 1 September 1871 and eventually to Greenwich Park in October 1888. By this time Greenwich as a destination had lost its importance and anyway was by now served

by faster, more direct trains on the South Eastern Railway line and faced further competition from cheap tram fares. With traffic dwindling, the line was closed in January 1917 as a war economy measure and never re-opened. The section of line between Nunhead and Lewisham Road was refurbished by the Southern Railway as part of its electrification scheme, and a new spur constructed to the Mid-Kent line. The branch beyond Lewisham Road, through Blackheath to Greenwich, was formally abandoned in 1929.

Shortly before the start of the Second World War the station building at Blackheath Hill was let to the Helliot Machine Tool Company, and the tunnel was in the hands of a builders' merchant who used it for the storage of concrete blocks and other materials. In July 1940 the tunnel was leased to Greenwich Council for use as an air-raid shelter for local residents. Alterations were made to the tunnel portals, a main access route from the road was provided via steps down from Sparta Street, and chemical toilets positioned near the entrance. Bunks were allocated to individual shelterers and provision made for personal possessions to be kept underground during daytime hours when the shelter would not normally be occupied. Special provisions were made to keep families together in the shelter rather than divide it into male and female dormitories as was the frequent practice elsewhere.

The tunnel was transferred back to the Southern Railway in December 1946 and it was then let to the Helliot Machine Tool Company (who already occupied the station building above) for use as a machine shop. Helliot left in 1958 and the tunnel remained vacant for several years. It was occupied for three years between 1966 and 1969 by another engineering firm, R. Taylor & Co, and was again left empty until 1975 when W. A. Storey (Plastics) Ltd took possession. The company, which occupied the site until 1986, manufactured road signs and was instrumental in the development of both standardised road signs for all of Britain's highways and also of the reflective coatings now used on all such signs.

In 1987 the station and surrounding area was acquired for housing development and shortly afterwards much demolition was undertaken. At that time the tunnel and approach cuttings were cleared to allow a safety and stability survey to be undertaken and the opportunity was taken to photograph and record what remained.

Left: What appears to be standard-gauge rails can be seen embedded into the concrete floor of the tunnel which, as we have seen on the previous page, was raised some four feet above the original rail level when the tunnel was converted for commercial use. It is probable that a convenient length of second-hand track was used to transfer heavy items between machine tools while being worked upon. This was common practice in many engineering workshops.

Left: The buried entrance to the shelter at Eothan School, uncovered during the redevelopment of the site in 1995.

Below: The flattened ovoid cross-section of the concrete tunnel shelter at Eothan School gives the structure immense strength. It appears to have been constructed from pre-cast concrete sections. Narrow wooden benches, fragments of which appear to be scattered across the floor, would have run down each side of the shelter.

Eothan School

In 1892 the sisters Catherine and Winifred Pye established a private school for girls in a house they had purchased in Eothan Close off Harestone Hill in Caterham. From an initial student roll of just eight girls the school gradually expanded and two nearby properties were purchased to provide boarding facilities and accommodation for a junior school. By 1934 the number of girls attending had increased to two hundred. Academically successful but dogged always by financial difficulties, management of the school eventually came under the control of the Church Schools Company, a charity set up to provide a church-based education for children from middle class families.

In 1995 Eothan merged with Caterham School, an independent school for boys. The Eothan Close site on Harestone Hill was no longer required and was quickly earmarked for mixed development of houses, flats and a health centre. While foundations were being excavated for the health centre, one of the school air-raid shelters was discovered, partly buried beneath a former tennis court.

Woldingham Village Green

Woldingham in east Surrey, a village just inside the M25 boundary with a population of a little over 2,250, was recognised as the second-richest suburb in Britain according to a survey carried out by the *Daily Telegraph* in December 2007. It is the home of the prestigious Woldingham Girls' School and during the Second World War was also home to an extensive military encampment and a secretive Czechoslovak military radio intelligence station. Beneath an innocuous manhole cover in the corner of the picturesque village green there lies buried a substantial concrete air-raid shelter.

Above: In a seemingly idyllic setting on the village green at Woldingham, a distinctly utilitarian steel manhole cover gives access to a Second World War air-raid shelter buried beneath the well-kept grass.
Right: Unlike the shelter at Eothan school, the Woldingham shelter was constructed in-situ with vertical side walls. The characteristic marks in the concrete made by the wooden shuttering can be clearly seen in this photograph.

Whitgift School

Whitgift is an independent school for boys that, since 1931, has been located at Haling Park in South Croydon, home in the sixteenth century to Lord Howard of Effingham. The school is set in some forty-five acres of parkland and is notable not just for its academic achievements but also for the range of wildlife to be found within its grounds.

During the Second World War a series of underground air-raid shelters were constructed to provide protection for the school's 200 students and staff. Unlike most shelters of this type, which were semi-underground concrete structures covered by a prominent earth mound, those at Whitgift School were completely buried beneath the lawns that surround the main building. Each with a capacity of approximately thirty occupants, the shelters are accessed via inconspicuous manholes and steeply inclined steel ladders at each end of the concrete

shelter tunnel. A small partitioned area at the base of the entry shaft contained a chemical toilet which, when the shelter was in use, would have been hidden by a sacking curtain to offer some degree of privacy. The shelter was provided with longitudinal wooden benches supported on concrete piers but, although the shelter appears to have survived in remarkably good condition, the timberwork has been removed.

Above: The unobtrusive entrance hatch giving access to one of the air-raid shelters at Whitgift School could easily be mistaken for a conventional sewer manhole cover.

Left: The interior of one of the Whitgift School shelters. The half-width wall at the far end partially encloses the entrance shaft and toilet cubicle. The concrete piers abutting the side walls once supported wooden benches that have long since disappeared.

Above: Preliminary work in hand to remove the turf and expose the blocked entrance to one of the underground air-raid shelters in Sunny Hill Park.

Sunny Hill Park, Hendon

As its name suggests, Sunny Hill Park is a pleasant public park extending over fifty acres of high, rolling ground above Hendon with extensive views to the north and west. In the late autumn of 1939, with war in the air, a series of trench shelters, now long disappeared, were built in the park, along with five underground shelters all of which have survived. The story of the Sunny Hill shelters is typical of the shelter-building arrangements of all the London boroughs, each of which was required to provide shelter accommodation for ten percent of its population; in the case of Hendon this represented 17,000 places. To fulfil this obligation a Home Office grant of £24,207 was made available to the council.

The Borough Council initially decided that their obligation would be fulfilled by providing trench shelters for 3,500 persons, underground concrete shelters (built by a commercial contractor) for 12,000, and 'shop' shelters for the remaining 1,500. The so-called 'shop' shelters are a little-known feature of Britain's Second World War air-raid precaution scheme. Essentially, local authorities were empowered to compulsorily acquire vacant shops and other commercial premises in residential areas and strengthen the basements and ground floors to provide ad hoc shelter accommodation for its residents.

During the early winter of 1939, with the war in Europe now underway but with England as yet largely unaffected, a problem arose

Above: The steps, just the top of which can be seen in the photograph opposite, have now been completely cleared to allow access to the shelter.

Above: A group of volunteers engaged in chipping away the concrete cap from the emergency exit shaft of the second of the Sunny Hill Park shelters to be opened up for investigation.

in the shelter-building programme. The huge increase in military building projects had led to a shortage in the supply of concrete while, somewhat bizarrely, the country was at the same time suffering a surfeit of bricks. At that time Hendon had so far completed 2,950 underground shelter spaces and 1,500 shop spaces and, in view of the difficulties with sourcing concrete, it was decided that the remaining places should be provided in the form of brick-built surface shelters.

Ultimately, brick shelters were ubiquitous but the majority were demolished at the end of the war, a task that was often not difficult because they tended to be poorly constructed using inferior mixes of cement. The more substantial underground shelters, however, have frequently survived although many, like those at Sunny Hill Park, now lie buried with their entrances thoroughly blocked up.

In July 2010 an exploratory dig was organised jointly by Hendon & District Archaeological Society, University College London Department of Archaeology, and Subterranea Britannica to investigate the Sunny Hill shelters, which lay beneath a patch of ground heavily overgrown with brambles and nettles. A row of five identical, parallel shelters was discovered and, given the limited time available for the dig, two were investigated. One was accessed via the main entrance which consisted of a flight of steps at the end of the long, narrow concrete structure, and the second via an emergency escape hatch at the innermost end of the shelter. The hatch had been sealed by a concrete cap which had to be laboriously chipped away to gain entry.

Above left: The emergency escape hatch cleared of its concrete cap, ready for access.

Above right: An interior view of the blocked main entrance staircase to the Sunny Hill shelter, access to which had been gained via the vertical emergency access shaft.

Left: Interior view of one of the Sunny Hill Park shelters showing the vertical steel ladder giving access to the emergency exit hatch. The brick partition at the far end conceals the shelter's toilet cubicle. Note the severe crack in the left-hand wall near the camera position and the narrower, floor-to-ceiling crack in the right-hand wall.

St. Leonard's Court, East Sheen

Above: This ornate structure, in a crossover Arts and Crafts / Deco Period architectural style, looking rather like a rural dovecote in a suburban setting, is in fact the entrance to an air-raid shelter for St Leonard's Court in East Sheen.

Above: A central access corridor runs through the shelter with a male day-room and dormitory to one side and female equivalents on the other. This is the Ladies' day room, complete with wooden benches and Elsan toilet cubicles at the far end. The shelter is currently used as a storeroom by the property maintenance firm looking after St Leonard's Court.

St. Leonard's Court is a stylish 1930s block of flats, set back from Sheen Lane in East Sheen. In 1939 a large air-raid shelter was built beneath the lawns that front the main building. Initially the shelter consisted of just two large rooms with benches, intended for short-term occupation by residents of the flats. In November 1940 work began on a major expansion of the shelter with two more rooms constructed in the space between the existing shelter and the flats. When completed, the original shelter was designated as day-rooms and the new section as night-time dormitories.

A similar shelter still survives (although in poor internal condition due to flooding) at Deanhill on Upper Richmond Road, opposite the junction of Clifford Avenue. It is rumoured that a third shelter of similar design was constructed on the site of the Courtlands Estate at the junction of Sheen Road and Queen's Road, and that it was destroyed, with considerable loss of life, by a German bomb in 1940. This, however, is unlikely as the only recorded bombing, which partially demolished Runnymede House on 20 September 1940, did not result in any fatalities.

Above left: A surviving Elsan chemical closet in one of the Ladies' toilet cubicles. The steel ladder gives access to an emergency escape hatch.

Above right: The night rooms are divided into eight bays, four either side of a central corridor. Each bay had three bunks mounted one above the other. Mattresses would have been put on wooden planks placed across the bricks seen protruding from the partition walls. Each bunk had a wooden shelf with its own light and light switch and the bunks are all numbered and provided with similarly numbered clothes hooks on the end of the bay walls. At the rear of the night rooms there are two escape hatches accessed by step irons set in the end walls.

Right: The base of the main entrance staircase, seen from the central spine corridor.

Clapton ARP Control Centre

Early in the Second World War every London borough established a control centre from which its air-raid warnings and the activities of its wardens could be co-ordinated. Similarly, Civil Defence Controls were set up to organise the rescue and welfare of air-raid victims. Some of these centres were established in the basements of town halls and others were purpose built on other council-owned properties such as maintenance yards or even on the perimeters of public parks. Although these premises fell into disuse at the end of the war, many were refurbished in the early 1950s to serve similar functions as Civil Defence Controls throughout the Cold War. Many boroughs took on their Cold War responsibilities with little enthusiasm and, consequently, the control centres remained largely unchanged from their wartime appearance. Two good examples, in Clapton and Hackney, are detailed below while others, including the large subterranean control centre at Southall, are included in the section of this book dedicated to Cold War bunkers.

Above: Access to the Clapton ARP centre, in Rossendale Road, was via a flight of five steps behind the door in the concrete wall between the black and yellow bins to the right of the photograph. At the bottom of the steps the bunker was sealed by a gas-tight door. The red brick building, now much altered, which surmounts the upper section of the concrete bunker was a wartime gas-decontamination centre.

Left: The main control room at Clapton. Although briefly reactivated in 1952 to perform a Cold War role as the Hackney Borough Sub-Control, the Clapton bunker has retained a number of original wartime artefacts including a couple of stretchers, hurricane lamps, an air-raid siren and a very ancient bicycle. Notice in this photograph the emergency exit hatch accessed by a short steel ladder.

Hackney ARP Control Centre

Right: The Hackney Second World War ARP Control Centre is located beneath the car park at Hackney Town Hall in Hillman Street. The entrance is a sloping-roofed concrete blockhouse in a corner of the car park. The bunker was reactivated in 1954 as Hackney Borough Control, but by 1964 it was so damp that it was unusable and Hackney Control was co-located with Stoke Newington Borough Control at Stoke Newington Town Hall.

Below left: The control room in the bunker is now used as a dumping ground for surplus furniture from the council offices, archived documents and a surprising number of old paraffin heaters. Notice the emergency escape hatch high up in the wall, a typical feature of this type of bunker.

Below right: 'Bicycle' powered Suttcliffe Speakman air filters in the ventilation plant room. Normally driven electrically, the filters could be operated manually using the pedal assemblies in event of a power failure.

Erith Hospital

Shortly before the First World War a new hospital was opened at the top of Park Crescent in Erith on land donated by a Mr Gunning, a local benefactor, to replace an earlier cottage hospital, built in 1871, on Crayford Road. In 1938 Erith Borough Council began the construction of an underground Civilian Casualty Station and Field Hospital adjacent to the main hospital building. The underground hospital, one of a large number of medical facilities established in the months leading up to the Second World War, was undertaken under the auspices of the Ministry of Health Emergency Medical Services in anticipation of the expected large-scale bombing casualties. There is documentary evidence to suggest that five other underground hospitals similar to that at Erith were planned in 1938 but none of the others appear to have been completed and their proposed locations are unknown.

The underground hospital consists of some fifty rooms and was originally divided into two sections, front and rear, which were mirror images of each other, one section for the treatment of male patients and the other for females. The building was constructed with rounded-arched ceilings, which made for a very strong structure, above which horizontal girders supported a concrete roof capped by a deep covering of earth. A notable feature of the interior arrangement was a long drainage gully in the floor intended to drain away water which had been used to hose-down patients contaminated with mustard gas.

In the late 1940s the modest X-ray department at Erith, in common with those at many other hospitals throughout the country, was being overwhelmed by demand due to the increasing prevalence of cases of tuberculosis that was sweeping the country. In 1950 it was decided that the underground hospital at Erith, which had lain disused since 1945, should be refurbished to house an expanded X-ray unit, its concrete construction making it ideal for this purpose, which it continues to fulfil to the present day.

Chapter 6

GOVERNMENT & MILITARY HEADQUARTERS

By the mid-1930s the British Government was sure that another major war was looming and, despite the general leaning towards a policy of appeasement, began to make preparations, if not for war, then at least for effective measures of passive defence. During those years military air power became increasingly significant and posed the most sinister threat to Britain's security. It was confidently predicted that within hours of the declaration of war the skies over London would blacken with German bombers, the capital would be obliterated, the seat of government destroyed and it would be the end of England and the end of the British Empire. London would become untenable and, as early as 1937, plans were under consideration for the evacuation of central government and the higher administration of the three fighting services to alternative accommodation far from central London. The Chiefs of Staff argued for evacuation to distant locations in the west country, but the cabinet decided, initially at least, to construct bomb-proof emergency accommodation within the Whitehall area.

Plans were drawn up, under the guidance and advice of the eminent consulting engineer Sir Harley Dalrymple-Hay, for the construction of a series of interconnected departmental bunkers in tunnels similar to those on the underground railways, buried one hundred feet beneath Whitehall. Dalrymple-Hay already had immense experience in tunnelling through the London clay in his role as resident engineer for the Waterloo and City Railway in 1894, as engineer to all the Yerkes underground lines during the years leading up to the First World War, and as consulting engineer to the Post Office underground railway. His scheme for Whitehall envisaged pairs of parallel, twenty-five-feet-diameter segmented-iron tube tunnels providing all the necessary office accommodation, with a twelve-feet-diameter interconnected access and service tunnel running between them. The twelve-feet tunnels would be extended to act as linking passages between the various departmental bunkers. Dalrymple-Hay estimated that the work would take two years to complete and would cost about £1,000,000.

The Whitehall tunnel scheme met with general approval but in

October 1939, with war looming, it was turned down on account of the cost and the potential shortage of the necessary material resources as government geared up for war production. Although the main proposals were rejected, a more modest scheme to construct a deep-level communications tunnel beneath Whitehall did go ahead in December 1939. Built under the authority of the General Post Office, the twelve-feet-diameter tunnel stretched from Trafalgar Square, beneath Whitehall telephone exchange in Craig's Court and along the length of Whitehall itself, beyond which, a later, smaller, eight-foot tunnel headed southwest to the Horseferry Road complex of the North and South Rotundas and the Steel Framed Building, described below. Although intended primarily as a GPO cable tunnel, later, a small number of lifts were installed at selected government buildings, which could in theory provide limited underground access between those buildings. The central section of the main tunnel was occupied by the GPO Q WHITEHALL private telephone exchange, whilst on the surface in Horse Guards Avenue was the FEDERAL telephone exchange. All of these telephone services were connected via another underground tunnel to the bomb resistant FARADAY exchange in Godliman Street, to the south of St. Paul's Cathedral.

With the original tunnel scheme now abandoned, a new series of bunkers was built. The Admiralty built a massive citadel on Horse Guards Parade independent of the Ministry of Works. They also built a standby facility in the grounds of the Admiralty Charts Depot in Oxgate Lane, Cricklewood. This consisted of a fortified basement and sub-basement containing control and communications facilities along with a ventilation plant room. Above this there was a three-storey office block built around a central courtyard. An almost identical building, known as STATION Z was constructed for the Air Ministry at the rear of HM Stationery Office at Headstone Drive Whealdstone. A proposed War Office bunker at Kneller Hall, Twickenham occupied by the Royal Army School of Music was not proceeded with.

Although an underground War Room in the Harrow area was

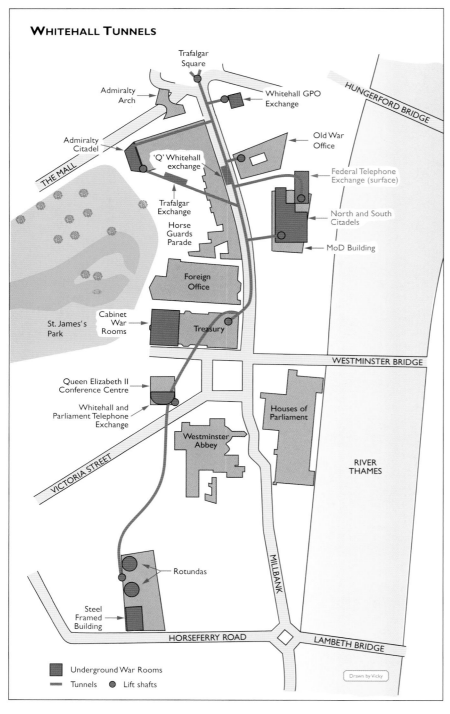

WHITEHALL TUNNELS

Trafalgar Square

Admiralty Arch

Whitehall GPO Exchange

HUNGERFORD BRIDGE

Admiralty Citadel

'Q' Whitehall exchange

Old War Office

THE MALL

Trafalgar Exchange

Federal Telephone Exchange (surface)

Horse Guards Parade

North and South Citadels

MoD Building

Foreign Office

St. James's Park

Cabinet War Rooms

Treasury

WESTMINSTER BRIDGE

Queen Elizabeth II Conference Centre

Houses of Parliament

Whitehall and Parliament Telephone Exchange

Westminster Abbey

VICTORIA STREET

RIVER THAMES

Rotundas

MILLBANK

Steel Framed Building

HORSEFERRY ROAD

LAMBETH BRIDGE

Drawn by Vicky

▪ Underground War Rooms
— Tunnels ● Lift shafts

proposed for the Ministry of Home Security in 1938, the plan was subsequently abandoned. The department was compelled to make do with accommodation in the strengthened basement of the Home Office building in Whitehall.

The War Cabinet War Room, known as PADDOCK, built beneath the Post Office Research Station at Dollis Hill, was commissioned in June 1941. Unlike the armed-forces war rooms, PADDOCK was surmounted by just a single-storey surface office block. For a number of reasons, including the logistical difficulties involved in transporting large numbers of staff to the suburbs, the effects this might have on morale, and the fact that the expected German aerial onslaught never fully materialised, the northwest London war rooms were soon seen as largely irrelevant encumbrances rather than valuable assets. Instead, it was decided that, in the interim at least, the government departments would remain in Whitehall for as long as possible, protected where necessary by emergency war rooms created in makeshift basement shelters. The most famous of these is the Cabinet War Rooms beneath the former Ministry of Works offices in Great George Street, which is now one of London's prime visitor attractions. The task of reinforcing the overhead cover of the Cabinet War Rooms in October 1940, some months before PADDOCK was completed, indicates that even at that early date the utility of the suburban bunkers was in doubt.

By the autumn of 1940 the Cabinet had made a firm decision that the seat of government would remain in Whitehall. Specifications were issued for the construction of a series of new, hardened war rooms including accommodation for the War Office, known colloquially as Montagu House Citadels North and South, beneath the now demolished annexe to the former Ministry of Labour offices in Montagu House. A further group of hardened citadels was constructed on the site of the London Gas Light and Coke Company's gasholders on a plot of land bounded by Great Peter Street, Monck Street, Marsham Street and Horseferry Road.

Above: The route of the GPO cable tunnel beneath Whitehall, which was constructed in the same way as a typical London Transport tube tunnel, and lined with standard cast-iron tunnel segments. FEDERAL exchange was demolished when the new MoD building was constructed and the cable tunnel was rerouted through the North and South Citadel bunkers beneath the new building. The Whitehall and Parliament telephone exchange was built below the Queen Elizabeth II Conference Centre in the early 1980s.

Above: Occupying a corner position at the junction of Edgware Road and Oxgate Lane, the frontage of the Admiralty Charts Establishment has an imposing presence with its bleak brick façade offset by an imposing Portland Stone portal to the entrance front.

OXGATE

The Admiralty Citadel is concealed beneath a late-1930s office building at the Naval Charts Factory, which had been established on land between Humber Road and Oxgate Lane, Cricklewood, in 1923. The site was identified as potentially suitable in 1937, construction commenced in the following year and the bunker was available for occupation in December 1939. The surface building was completed in 1940. As at PADDOCK, which was less than a mile away, senior staff were housed in requisitioned flats in Nevilles Court while it was planned that more junior staff and clerks would be accommodated in nearby schools which, it was assumed, would be rendered redundant by evacuation at the start of the war.

The bunker was a two-storey construction built as a large rectangular box with the intermediate floor and the upper storey roof supported by twenty-five evenly-spaced concrete pillars. Within the rectangular box, individual rooms were separated by lightweight partition walls. The lower floor contained all the service plant including air-conditioning and ventilation equipment, and an emergency generator.

By 1943, with the threat of German bombing having receded to insignificance, the importance of the OXGATE bunker declined and much of its function was transferred to ADMIRALTY BLOCKHOUSE on Horse Guards Parade. The facility was closed down completely at the end of 1944. In more recent years Oxgate Lane was occupied by the Health & Safety Executive, but the building is currently in private hands and used as a carpet warehouse.

Above: Looking down the main western stairs from the upper to the lower floor of the bunker. This photograph was taken in 2001 before the lower floor was pumped dry. The water can be seen just below the top of the blast door. Crates of air filters can be seen on the concrete shelf above the stairs.

Above right: Two spiral staircases provided emergency exit routes from the lower floor of the bunker. This view of the upper landing of the south staircase illustrates the thickness of the concrete floor slab between the upper and lower levels.

Below right: The bottom of the ornate, cast-iron spiral staircase in the western emergency exit shaft.

Above: The lower floor of the Oxgate bunker, devoid of plant and internal partitions although sections of ventilation duct remain suspended from the ceiling. Note the massive concrete pillars supporting the upper floor of the bunker and the building above.

Above left: The blast door at the bottom of the western spiral staircase. The corrosion is a consequence of the lower floor having been under water for a prolonged period.

Above right: Control gear for the standby generator, with powerhouse ventilation ducting above.

Left: The upper floor of the bunker, in use as a carpet warehouse. When this photograph was taken the lower floor was submerged in stagnant seepage water.

Left: The anonymous, single-storey red-brick office block that stood above the War Cabinet War Room at Dollis Hill. The tall ventilation tower at the end of the building, with its high-level, louvred air ducts, was, perhaps, a clue that there was more to this structure than was obvious at first sight.

Below: A view down the spiral emergency escape staircase at the south end of the bunker.

PADDOCK

The General Post Office established a research station at Dollis Hill in 1921 and it was here, in 1943, that Colossus, the world's first electronic computer was developed – later to be installed at Bletchley Park and used to break the German Lorenz code. Some years earlier however, in 1938, the site was identified as a suitable location for a dispersed War Cabinet War Room remote from the dangers of bombing in central London. The specific site chosen was an area of ground on the perimeter of the Post Office site parallel with Brook Street. The forty-feet-deep excavations for the two-storey underground structure began in October 1938 and the bunker was ready for occupation in June 1940. No dormitory space was provided for the working complement of 200 men and women. Instead, senior staff were allocated sixty requisitioned luxury flats in Nevilles Court in Dollis Lane, approximately 200 yards from PADDOCK, while the more lowly clerks and typists were billeted in nearby school buildings.

PADDOCK appears to have aroused Churchill's personal animosity and was not a success. The War Cabinet met there only twice, the first time on 3 October 1940, the second and last on 10 March 1941. Criticising the facilities at Dollis Hill, Churchill wrote to the Cabinet Secretary, Edward Bridges, shortly after the first meeting:

'The accommodation at PADDOCK is quite unsuited to the conditions that have arisen.'

Later he minuted Bridges that:

'The War Cabinet cannot live and work there for weeks on end … PADDOCK should be treated as a last resort.'

PADDOCK

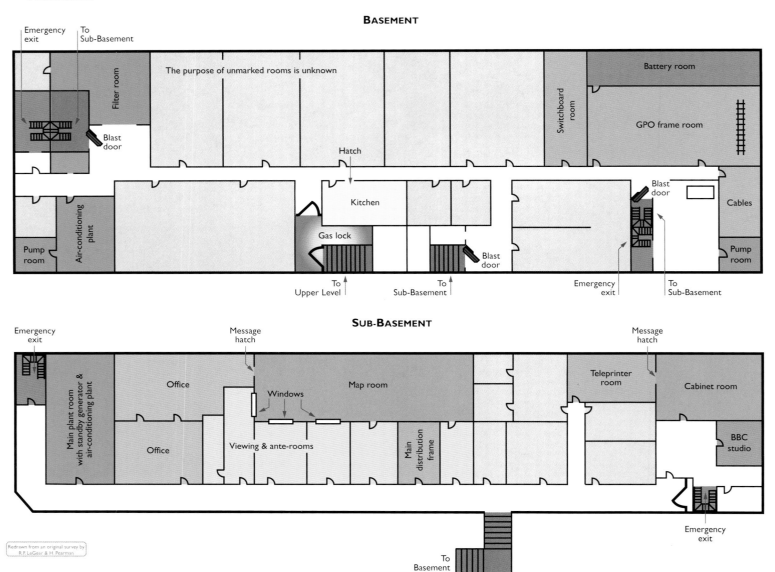

BASEMENT

Emergency exit

To Sub-Basement

Filter room

The purpose of unmarked rooms is unknown

Battery room

Switchboard room

GPO frame room

Blast door

Hatch

Kitchen

Gas lock

Air-conditioning plant

Pump room

Blast door

Cables

Pump room

Emergency exit

To Upper Level

To Sub-Basement

Blast door

Emergency exit

To Sub-Basement

SUB-BASEMENT

Emergency exit

Message hatch

Message hatch

Main plant room with standby generator & air-conditioning plant

Office

Windows

Map room

Teleprinter room

Cabinet room

Office

Viewing & ante-rooms

Main distribution frame

BBC studio

Emergency exit

To Basement

Redrawn from an original survey by R. F. LeGear & H. Pearman

The bunker remained disused after the final cabinet meeting in March 1941 although a security presence was maintained until 1944 when the site was abandoned. The surface building was subsequently into the GPO's research complex, the upper floor of the underground bunker seeing occasional use as a recreational facility. The whole site was vacated by the Post Office in 1976 and has been redeveloped as an industrial and residential complex. The underground bunker was briefly considered for use as an emergency war room for the north London group of boroughs in 1981 but was rejected when it was discovered that the lower floor suffered from a serious ingress of seepage water. The part of the site that includes PADDOCK was acquired in May 1997 by the Network Housing Group and one of the planning conditions imposed by Brent Council was that the bunker should be made safe, kept clear of water and be opened to the public on at least two days each year. These immensely popular regular openings are guided by members of Subterranea Britannica

Above: The map room, on the lower floor of the bunker, seen here in April 2001 shortly after some two feet of flood water had been pumped out.

Above: The map room in April 2001 before the flood water was pumped out.

Below: Air-conditioning equipment in the upper-floor plant room.

Above: The Cabinet Room at PADDOCK, where Winston Churchill chaired a meeting of the War Cabinet on 3 October 1940.

Below: The generator room, after the flood water had been pumped out.

Above: The upper-basement spine corridor. Note the serving hatch from the kitchen on the left. The sign in the middle distance reading 'Floor 28' is, rather confusingly, pointing to the stairs up to the surface building above. This dates from the 1950s when the floors of all buildings were consecutively numbered by the GPO. Hence the two-level bunker with its single floor building above ground became floors 26-28.

STATION 'Z'

Similar in design to the Admiralty Citadel in Cricklewood, the Air Ministry war room, known cryptically as STATION 'Z', was, as we have already learned, built beneath the courtyard of the HMSO printing works on Headstone Drive at Wealdstone in Middlesex. Construction started in 1938 and the bunker was ready for occupation in October 1940. The role and scope of the Air Ministry expanded exponentially throughout the Second World War and increased in importance in the post-war years as it took command of the nuclear deterrent, a responsibility it handed over to the Royal Navy in June 1969. The expanded wartime role required additional administrative accommodation resulting in the Air Ministry occupying a substantial segment of the Rotunda complex in Horseferry Road, described elsewhere in this section.

The Air Ministry remained at Cricklewood until 1955 when the site was handed over to the Home Office Directorate of Communications which was responsible for, amongst other things, the Civil Defence Radio Network and the Hilltop Radio System, both of which were important elements in the plans for the continuity of government in the event of nuclear war. The prominent radio antenna in the station's inner forecourt was erected at that time. In 1966 the bunker was earmarked as a temporary home for the regional government bunker (Sub-Regional Control 6.2) that would oversee the governance of

Above left: This aerial view shows the open quadrangle, enclosed by a three-storey office block, which together with the two-level bunker below ground comprises STATION Z.

Above right: The Air Ministry citadel lies beneath the courtyard in the foreground. Two ventilation stacks rise from the bunker on each side of the central bay of the surface office. The aerial mast to the left is a feature of the later Home Office occupancy of the site.

Below: Layout plan of the lower floor of the Cricklewood bunker.

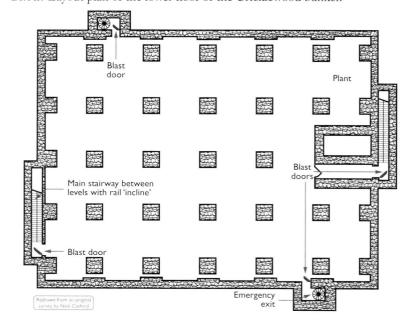

Berkshire and Buckinghamshire, along with north and west London, should the country come under nuclear attack by the Soviet Union. This scheme was overtaken by the lessening of international tension from the late 1960s and the run down in Civil Defence expenditure. By the 1980s the site was once again firmly in the hands of the Home Office radio department. The government finally gave up the site in 1992 and the surface building was demolished in 1996. The bunker still survives under the ownership of the Kodak company, which purchased the site for expansion of its adjacent premises, but is not currently used although it is kept secure and ventilated.

Above right: Note the trough rails mounted on the stairs between the upper and lower level of the bunker. A specially adapted truck *(below right)*, with a triangular framework allowing the loading platform to remain horizontal on the incline, was used to winch goods and documents between floors.

Below: Looking out from the upper-floor plant access loading-bay into the main area of the bunker. By 2005, when this photograph was taken, all the blast doors and other major fittings had been removed.

Above: Concrete foundation blocks for the air-conditioning plant on the lower floor of the bunker. No trace of any of the plant or electrical services now remain.

Above: The Admiralty Citadel, described by Prime Minister Winston Churchill as 'a vast monstrosity which weighs upon the Horse Guards Parade'. Note the pillbox built into the top right corner.

Admiralty Citadel

The monolithic bunker on Horse Guards Parade, its intimidating outline now softened by Virginia creeper, was built in 1940 and brought into use before completion in 1941 to accommodate the Operational Intelligence Centre (OIC), re-located from the unprotected basement of the adjacent Old Admiralty building.

The Citadel provided protection for the OIC, the Submarine Tracking Room, Trade Plot, Central War Registry and communications facilities on the lower floor (only partially semi-sunk to match the levels of the Old Admiralty Building). The upper floor contained conference and toilet facilities and dormitories. Mounted on the heavily reinforced roof were air conditioning/filtering equipment and generators. After this complex became operational the reserve bunker at Oxgate Lane, Cricklewood continued in this role. Some 600 personnel were employed within the Citadel.

Above: The upper storey of the south Rotunda. The pyramidical structure on the roof of the Rotunda incorporates part of the air-conditioning plant, while the rectangular building constructed partly on a cantilevered platform to the left houses an auxiliary generating set.

The Horseferry Rotundas

The Westminster Gas Light and Coke Company established a gasworks in Horseferry Road, Westminster in 1812. Although gas production at Horseferry Road ceased in 1875 following the construction of the company's huge new gasworks at Beckton in East London, the site was retained and housed by two very large, circular gasholders. These were demolished in 1937, leaving two sixty-feet-deep circular pits on the site. Immediately before the start of the Second World War the gas company made preparations to erect a new headquarters building of steel-framed construction on the southern edge of the compound facing Monck Street. Early in 1940 however, before work had proceeded far, the whole site was requisitioned by the government for the construction of alternative, bomb-proof accommodation for the Air Ministry. Erection of the five-storey steel-framed building went ahead, with the basement and ground floors reinforced as a blockhouse capable of surviving the effects of a 1,000lb bomb. Meanwhile, in November 1940, the contractors John Mowlem & Company started work on a vast, reinforced concrete bomb-proof circular citadel in the northern gasholder pit while Higgs & Hill Ltd began construction of a similar

bunker in the south pit. Both Rotundas consisted of three floors, one-and-a-half of which were completely underground with the above-ground sections protected by massively thick concrete walls and by roofs formed from no less than twelve feet of reinforced concrete. Construction was largely completed by June 1941 but it appears that the Air Ministry did not take up occupation until early the following year as the communications facilities were not completed until the end of December 1941.

The Horseferry Road complex was built on a lavish scale, with accommodation for a staff of 2,000. It was fully gas-proofed with a sophisticated ventilation and air-filtration plant, and had its own secure water supply from an artesian well. A six-megawatt generating station in the basement of the south Rotunda consisting of four Brush alternators driven by four 1,500 horsepower Petter diesel engines,

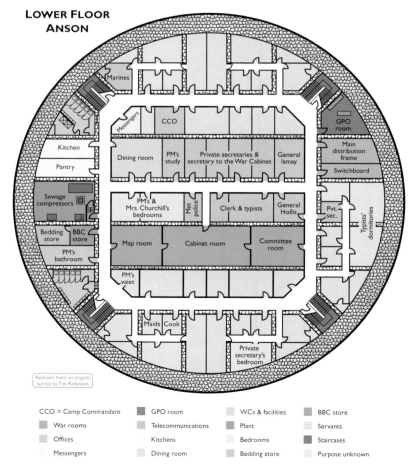

LOWER FLOOR ANSON

Redrawn from an original survey by Tim Robinson

CCO = Camp Commandant		
War rooms	GPO room	WCs & facilities	BBC store
Offices	Telecommunications	Plant	Servants
Messengers	Kitchens	Bedrooms	Staircases
	Dining room	Bedding store	Purpose unknown

Above: Layout diagram of the ANSON bunker on the lower floor of the north Rotunda.

Above: This curved passageway, known as The Crescent, was situated on the lower floor of the South Rotunda near the fuel storage tanks. Its shape reflects the circular outer wall of the bunker.

could cover the full load of the headquarters in event of a mains power failure. The basement also housed an extensive communication facility including a thirty-position manual telephone switchboard, teleprinters, radio communications equipment and cypher machines.

Although built primarily for the Air Ministry, the Rotundas and the Blockhouse were home to a rather fluid range of occupants during the progress of the war. Initially the Air Ministry occupied the Blockhouse and much of the other available space, but in October 1942 the majority of the north Rotunda and the upper floor of the south Rotunda were handed over to the War Office for the use of GHQ Land Forces and 21 Army Group, the Air Ministry contingent previously there retreating to the Blockhouse. Meanwhile, the Ministry of Home Security established its central war room in the north Rotunda. The threat of the German 'V1' flying bombs

and, more urgently, of the 'V2' missiles, resulted in the Air Ministry extending its occupancy of the south Rotunda while the basement of the north Rotunda was earmarked for use as a reserve Cabinet War Room. The Cabinet War Room facility, codenamed ANSON, occupied the whole of the bottom floor of the north Rotunda and included working, living and sleeping space for Prime Minister Winston Churchill and his wife, the Prime Minister's staff and the War Cabinet. Churchill, it would appear, was as unwilling to use ANSON as he had been PADDOCK earlier in the war and it is probable that ANSON was never fully utilised.

By the early 1950s the north Rotunda had been re-equipped to function as the Home Security War Room. In the event of war

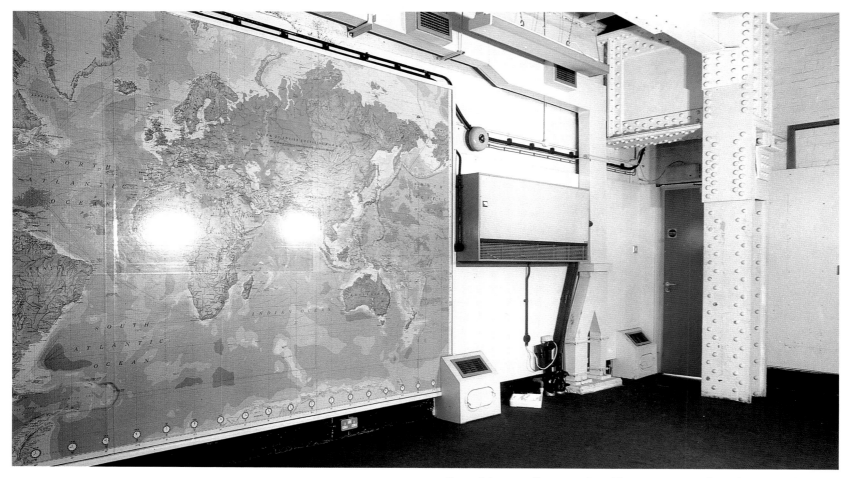

Above: A large, wall-mounted world map, a survivor from the 1990s when the building was in use as a naval communications centre, in a conference room in the Steel Framed Building. Notice the massive dimensions of the riveted steel girders which reinforce this structure, rendering it virtually bomb-proof.

with the Soviet Union, whether conventional or atomic, the north Rotunda would have acted as a central communications hub for a network of thirteen Regional War Rooms spread throughout the country. At that time it was envisaged that a Soviet attack, even using atomic bombs, would have consequences similar, though more intense, than those resulting from the worst conventional bombing of the Second World War. City centres and military installations, the assumed targets, might be completely destroyed but the majority of the country and even the suburbs of the larger conurbations, would be relatively unscathed. The Regional War Room concept was based upon the probability that, even if London and the seat of government were not destroyed, there might be severe communications dislocation and contact with the central administration could be restricted or lost for some time. Under these circumstances Regional Commissioners located in the Regional War Rooms would assume much of the responsibility for many aspects of central government

until communication was restored. Thereafter, general directions to the regions would be issued from the Home Security War Room and information from the regions would be collected and collated there. The Regional War Rooms were, however, seen essentially as little more than sophisticated Civil Defence Control Centres; their principal task was the rescue and recovery of survivors and the co-ordination of essential services, much as had been the role of the Civil Defence Corps during the Second World War. It was expected that in the aftermath of an atomic attack, survivors would be picked from the wreckage of their houses, they would be given a cup of tea, bulldozers would clear the rubble from the streets, men from the water and gas boards would re-connect the pipes and life would resume more-or-less as normal.

Above left: The entrance blast-door to the north Rotunda.

Above right: The corridor linking the Steel Framed Building to the south Rotunda. The distortion to the ceiling and right-hand wall was caused by a near miss from a V1 flying bomb during the Second World War.

Below right: Heating plant in the basement of the south Rotunda.

Above: Demolition of the Rotundas underway in March 2003. The vast scale of the buildings and the thickness of the concrete roof are clearly evident in this photograph.

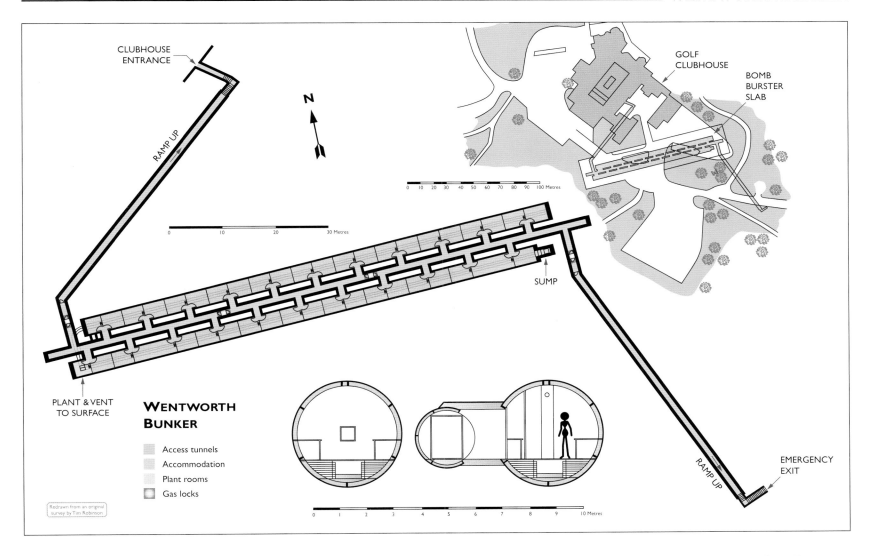

CLUBHOUSE ENTRANCE

RAMP UP

N

GOLF CLUBHOUSE

BOMB BURSTER SLAB

0 10 20 30 40 50 60 70 80 90 100 Metres

SUMP

0 10 20 30 Metres

PLANT & VENT TO SURFACE

WENTWORTH BUNKER

▒ Access tunnels
▒ Accommodation
▒ Plant rooms
▣ Gas locks

Redrawn from an original survey by Tim Robinson

RAMP UP

EMERGENCY EXIT

0 1 2 3 4 5 6 7 8 9 10 Metres

Wentworth Communications Bunker

Although Harley Dalrymple-Hay's proposal for deep-level bunkers beneath Whitehall was not accepted, his design *was* utilised, albeit on a smaller scale, beneath the forecourt of Wentworth House at Virginia Water which, since 1926, had been the clubhouse and administrative headquarters of the world-famous Wentworth Golf Club. Many researchers have, in fact, suggested that the Wentworth bunker was a trial run for the proposed but ultimately abortive Whitehall scheme, although the exact chronology of its planning and construction has not been established. It would appear that Wentworth was requisitioned, along with countless other country houses, at or shortly after the outbreak of war in 1939, and that

construction of the tunnels began shortly thereafter. It seems, however, that the house and tunnels remained unoccupied until the winter of 1940, when they were occupied by GHQ Home Forces.

Via a Command and District hierarchy, GHQ Home Forces controlled Britain's home defence force, tasked with resisting a German invasion in the first period of the Second World War, and also overseeing the training of the military units that would eventually re-occupy Europe after D-day. Following the outbreak of war GHQ Home Forces, along with its one-thousand-strong communications section, (No.1 HQ Signals Regiment), took up residence in St. Paul's School in Hammersmith. The school was badly damaged by enemy bombs during the London Blitz and, more importantly, severe damage was done to a vital telecommunications link; damage

Above: The now demolished emergency exit, which stood beside the drive leading to Wentworth House.

Above: A view from the central access corridor into one of the office tunnels, showing a vertical partition wall. The floors, which have been removed, were laid upon the brick dwarf walls, the space below forming a ventilation duct.
Below: The inclined passageway up to the emergency exit seen above left.

to a cable junction adjacent to Cadeby Hall, at Shepherds Bush, completely severed communications between St. Paul's School and the pivotal FARADAY telephone exchange. The bombing exposed the vulnerability of GHQ Home Forces' Hammersmith location, resulting in its rapid evacuation to Wentworth where the Headquarters administration section occupied the main house and several other nearby properties while No.1 Signals Regiment established itself in the recently completed tunnels.

Towards the end of 1943, with London now relatively safe from enemy bombing, GHQ Home Forces returned to St. Paul's School. Wentworth, meanwhile, became the Rear Headquarters of SHAEF, the Supreme Headquarters, Allied Expeditionary Force which was the overall Allied command for the military invasion of Europe. The main operational SHAEF headquarters was located at HMS Dryad at Southwick Park on Portsdown Hill overlooking Portsmouth harbour, while Wentworth was home to the rear support and administrative functions. Following the successful occupation of Europe SHAEF, along with its support units, was transferred to the European mainland, first to the Trianon Palace Hotel in Versailles and then, on 26 April 1945, to Frankfurt.

The Wentworth bunker, unused since December 1944, consists of two parallel, twenty-five-feet diameter iron-lined tubes approximately three-hundred-feet in length, with a smaller diameter pedestrian and service tunnel running between them. It is located deep beneath a large, rectangular concrete 'bomb-burster slab' a little to the south elevation of Wentworth House, the slab now forming the major part of the clubhouse car park. From the west end of the bunker the central

access tunnel turns sharply to the north and continues as a one-hundred metre-long inclined access passage which links, by means of a brick-built covered walkway, to the house. A similar passageway leads diagonally from the east end of the bunker to surface at small concrete emergency exit blockhouse adjacent to Wentworth Drive.

Above: The air lock at the east end of the bunker where the central corridor joins the emergency escape passage. The blast doors here are missing, presumably sent for scrap after the war.

South Kensington London Region Home Defence Control Centre

Although not strictly an underground structure, the South Kensington bunker deserves a mention here as it is a little-known structure that played a key role in co-ordinating all the Civil Defence measures in the London area throughout the Second World War. Prior to the outbreak of war, in order to manage the inevitable social dislocation that would result from the anticipated enemy bombing campaign, the country was divided into twelve Civil Defence regions, each under the control of a commissioner responsible to a newly-formed Ministry of Home Security. London was designated No.5 Region and its control headquarters was located in a purpose-built concrete bunker in front of the Geological Museum and adjacent to the Natural History Museum in South Kensington.

At the end of the war the control room was closed down and the building abandoned and sealed. It was to remain in this state until 1976 when the land upon which it stood was required for an extension to the Natural History Museum. When attempts were made to demolish the wartime structure it was discovered that the concrete walls were six feet thick and the cost would be prohibitive. The bunker was therefore incorporated within the new structure with its rear wall, the only section open to view, clad in brickwork along the building line of the new extension in order that it should blend seamlessly into the elevation. The two larger rooms within the bunker have been refurbished and are now used to store palaeontological specimens.

Left: One of the two former control rooms in the South Kensington bunker, now fitted out with modern storage units by the Natural History Museum.

Chapter 7

RAF FIGHTER COMMAND BUNKERS

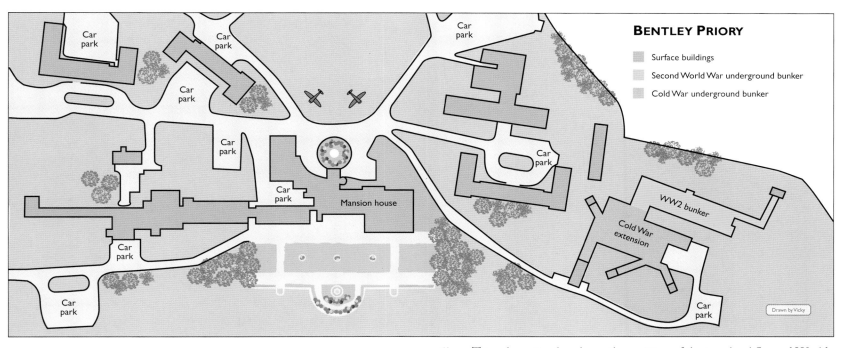

BENTLEY PRIORY

- Surface buildings
- Second World War underground bunker
- Cold War underground bunker

Car park

Mansion house

WW2 bunker

Cold War extension

Drawn by Vicky

Above: This schematic plan shows the position of the two-level Second World War underground bunker and the single-level Cold War extension at Bentley Priory in relation to the main house.

Air Defence of Great Britain

Throughout the Second World War the air defence of the UK was largely in the hands of RAF Fighter Command, and was co-ordinated from its headquarters at Bentley Priory near Stanmore in Middlesex. For control purposes Britain's fighter airfields were divided into four regional groups, each with its own underground Group operations room. Airfields in the southwest comprised No.10 Group and were controlled from an operations room deep underground at Box in Wiltshire; No.12 Group's airfields in the Midlands were controlled from an operations room at Watnall near Nottingham, and those in the north of the country from No.13 Group Headquarters at Kenton Bar near Newcastle. The fighter airfields that protected London and the southeast formed No.11 Group, whose operations room was housed in an underground bunker at Uxbridge.

Bentley Priory

The mansion house at Bentley Priory was acquired by the Air Ministry in 1926 and ten years later, in 1936, it became the headquarters of the newly formed Fighter Command. At the start of the Second World War a large, two-level control centre was constructed at a depth of forty feet below the lawn fronting the house. The underground operations room became operational in 1940. Its function was to filter and assess information regarding enemy air activity over the whole of Britain, received from radar stations, the numerous Royal Observer Corps observation posts and other miscellaneous sources, to generate an accurate overall picture of the current air threat. Information received at Bentley Priority from the four Group Headquarters and

from Anti-Aircraft Command provided a picture of the resources available to counter any threat encountered, and this, together with meteorological information, allowed Bentley Priory to co-ordinate air defence activity nationwide.

Bentley Priory's role continued in a modified form into the Cold War. In 1953 the site became the Air Defence Operations Centre (ADOC) for both Fighter and Bomber Commands. Following the formation of Strike Command in 1968 a new operations centre was established at High Wycombe. Subsequently the ADOC at Bentley Priory was run down, closing in 1971. In 1979 plans were prepared for a new UKAIR Permanent Static War Headquarters at High Wycombe. It was decided that this new control centre required an alternative reserve facility and that to provide this, the Bentley Priory bunker, which had been mothballed under care and maintenance for several years, should be refurbished and extended. The bunker was re-commissioned in its new role in 1990 but, in the face of changing defence priorities, was permanently closed in 2008. In September 2010 planning permission was granted for redevelopment of the site that included demolition of the bunker. The photographs that follow show Bentley Priory operations centre in its Cold War, guise.

Above: The main entrance to the extended Cold War bunker at Bentley Priory.
Below: The picquet post, or security office, inside the entrance building seen above, guarding the stairway to the bunker below.

Above: The base of the main access stairs. At the end of the corridor ahead, the passage turns right towards the original two-level control centre, and left into the new plant-room complex.

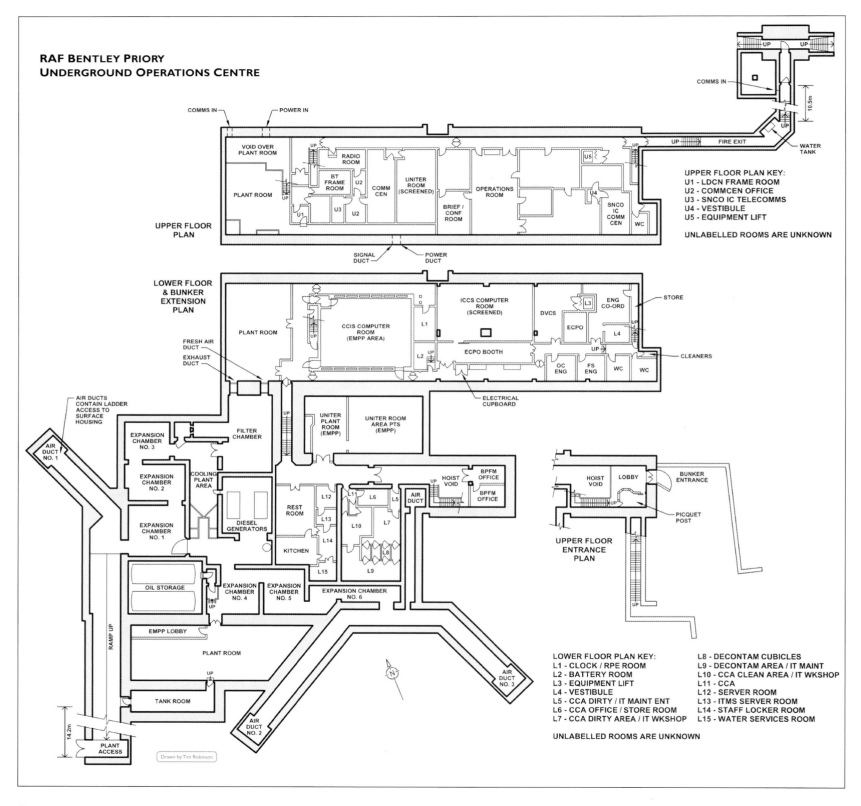

RAF BENTLEY PRIORY
UNDERGROUND OPERATIONS CENTRE

COMMS IN

UPPER FLOOR PLAN KEY:
U1 - LDCN FRAME ROOM
U2 - COMMCEN OFFICE
U3 - SNCO IC TELECOMMS
U4 - VESTIBULE
U5 - EQUIPMENT LIFT

UNLABELLED ROOMS ARE UNKNOWN

COMMS IN — POWER IN

UPPER FLOOR
PLAN

VOID OVER
PLANT ROOM
PLANT ROOM
BT FRAME ROOM
RADIO ROOM
U2
U1
U3
U2
COMM CEN
UNITER ROOM (SCREENED)
BRIEF / CONF ROOM
OPERATIONS ROOM
U5
U4
SNCO IC COMM CEN
WC
UP — FIRE EXIT
WATER TANK
10.5m

SIGNAL DUCT — POWER DUCT

LOWER FLOOR & BUNKER EXTENSION PLAN

FRESH AIR DUCT
EXHAUST DUCT

AIR DUCTS CONTAIN LADDER ACCESS TO SURFACE HOUSING

AIR DUCT NO. 1

PLANT ROOM
CCIS COMPUTER ROOM (EMPP AREA)
L1
L2
ICCS COMPUTER ROOM (SCREENED)
ECPO BOOTH
DVCS
ECPO
L3
L4
ENG CO-ORD
STORE
OC ENG
FS ENG
WC
WC
CLEANERS

ELECTRICAL CUPBOARD

EXPANSION CHAMBER NO. 3
EXPANSION CHAMBER NO. 2
EXPANSION CHAMBER NO. 1
COOLING PLANT AREA
FILTER CHAMBER
DIESEL GENERATORS
KITCHEN
REST ROOM
L12
L13
L14
L15
L11
L10
L9
L6
L5
L7
L8
UNITER PLANT ROOM (EMPP)
UNITER ROOM AREA PTS (EMPP)
AIR DUCT
HOIST VOID
BPFM OFFICE
BPFM OFFICE

HOIST VOID
LOBBY
BUNKER ENTRANCE
PICQUET POST

UPPER FLOOR ENTRANCE PLAN

OIL STORAGE
EXPANSION CHAMBER NO. 4
EXPANSION CHAMBER NO. 5
EXPANSION CHAMBER NO. 6

EMPP LOBBY
PLANT ROOM
TANK ROOM
RAMP UP
14.2m
PLANT ACCESS

AIR DUCT NO. 2
AIR DUCT NO. 3

N

Drawn by Tim Robinson

LOWER FLOOR PLAN KEY:
L1 - CLOCK / RPE ROOM
L2 - BATTERY ROOM
L3 - EQUIPMENT LIFT
L4 - VESTIBULE
L5 - CCA DIRTY / IT MAINT ENT
L6 - CCA OFFICE / STORE ROOM
L7 - CCA DIRTY AREA / IT WKSHOP

L8 - DECONTAM CUBICLES
L9 - DECONTAM AREA / IT MAINT
L10 - CCA CLEAN AREA / IT WKSHOP
L11 - CCA
L12 - SERVER ROOM
L13 - ITMS SERVER ROOM
L14 - STAFF LOCKER ROOM
L15 - WATER SERVICES ROOM

UNLABELLED ROOMS ARE UNKNOWN

Above: A view through the massive blast-doors securing the bunker, along the main access corridor towards the principal staircase and hoist void.

Above: The main Operations Room on the upper floor of the old bunker. Note the access control console in the centre of the right hand wall. This allowed manual override of a largely automated system that ensured that doors in the access air-locks were opened and closed in the correct sequence to ensure that a positive pressure was maintained within the bunker in order to avoid the risk of inducting contaminated air.

Left: The UNITER plant room and, up the steps, the main UNITER equipment hall. UNITER is a secure and survivable fixed communications network used by the RAF and introduced in two stages from 1988. The first stage consisted of a voice communications network linking fourteen nodes with the United Kingdom Air Defence Ground Environment (UKADGE). The second, implemented between 1991 and 1996, was a voice and data network linking fifty key RAF locations.

Above: The view from the UNITER hall looking down into the associated plant room. Both rooms have full Electro-Magnetic Pulse protection.

Below left: A standby generator in the new plant room.
Below right: The rather sinister engine exhaust duct above the plant room.

Above: Part of the highly sophisticated air-conditioning system installed in the Bentley Priory bunker.

RAF Uxbridge

No.11 Group's operations room at Uxbridge was built sixty feet beneath the lawns of Hillingdon House, which had been acquired for use as a military hospital during the First World War. In 1917 RAF Uxbridge (a non-flying site) was established in the grounds and during the Second World War the house became the headquarters of No.11 Group. It was also the headquarters of the Observer Corps between 1929 and 1936, after which the organisation relocated to Bentley Priory. Work on the underground operations room began in 1938 and it became operational on 25 August 1939. The bunker exercised control over seven Sector airfields at Tangmere, Kenley, Biggin Hill, Hornchurch, North Weald, Debden and Northolt, along with their satellite stations at Westhampnett, Croydon, West Malling, Lympe, Hawkinge, Gravesend, Rochford, Martlesham Heath and Stapleford Tawney. These were the airfields from which the Hurricanes and Spitfires that fought the Battle of Britain flew, and it is its historic controlling role in the autumn of 1940 that gave the Uxbridge bunker lasting fame as the Battle of Britain Operations Room.

Above: The unobtrusive emergency exit from the underground operations room at RAF Uxbridge. From behind the heavy steel blast doors, steps descend to the bunker sixty feet below ground.

Left: This view of the Operations Room at RAF Uxbridge shows the plotting table, overlooked by the controllers' gallery which is fronted by curved Perspex panels to reduce reflection from the lights below. The lower wooden gallery accommodated communications staff.

Above: The plotting table, viewed from the controllers' gallery above. The table consists of a large map of the Channel and southeast England, marked with all the RAF airfields and the Group and Sector boundaries. Flagged wooden tallies show the positions of the various RAF fighter squadrons and the tracks of incoming enemy formations. On the rear wall are the tote boards, one for each sector airfield, showing the state of all aircraft within the group by means of backlit panels.

Chapter 8

RAILWAY CONTROL CENTRES

In war, communication, in all its forms, is of vital importance We have seen already the measures taken during both the Second World War and the Cold War by the GPO to safeguard the telecommunications system. Similar measures were taken during both periods to maintain, as far as possible, an operable railway transport system. London Transport and all of the 'Big Four' railway companies, (Southern, Great Western, London & North Eastern and London Midland & Scottish), established wartime emergency control and communications centres and Air Raid Precautions control centres. The Great Western, for example, provided a comprehensive ARP control and emergency telephone switchboard in the bowels of Paddington station, all traces of which have now disappeared. Much

of the Southern Railway Company's emergency facilities, however, have survived to the present day.

In 1939 the Southern Railway took over the Deepdene Hotel near Dorking in Surrey for use as an emergency wartime headquarters as a precaution in case their vulnerable central London premises at Waterloo were destroyed. In the grounds of the hotel they took advantage of an existing network of natural caves which were extended and adapted to provide protected accommodation for the headquarters telephone exchange and the network traffic control centre. In addition to the main control centre at Deepdene, the company also built three smaller, divisional emergency control centres at Woking, Orpington and Redhill.

Deepdene

The Deepdene control centre was accessed via three entrances into the hillside and a sixty-feet-deep vertical emergency exit shaft at the innermost end of the tunnel complex. A staff of approximately thirty men and women manned the centre on a permanent basis, with representatives from the Motive Power department, the Chief Electrical and Mechanical engineers' departments and from the Train Operating department. The underground accommodation consists of fourteen interlinked rooms, most of which have been stripped of their fixtures and fittings so it is difficult to accurately identify every room's allocated function. It is known that at least one and possibly two dormitories were provided for staff, and that a separate combined office and bedroom was allocated to the night duty officer. Surprisingly, the underground complex remained operation through the early Cold War years until the mid-1960s when British Railways vacated Deepdene House. The house was demolished in 1969 and an ugly modern office block now stands on the site.

Left: The eastern, or No.3, entrance to the Deepdene railway control bunker. This entrance leads directly to the battery room and thence into the bunker's telephone exchange.

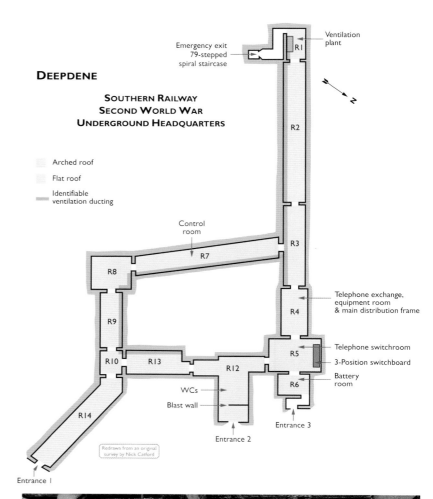

DEEPDENE

SOUTHERN RAILWAY
SECOND WORLD WAR
UNDERGROUND HEADQUARTERS

Arched roof

Flat roof

Identifiable ventilation ducting

Ventilation plant

Emergency exit 79-stepped spiral staircase

R1

R2

Control room

R7

R3

R8

Telephone exchange, equipment room & main distribution frame

R4

R9

Telephone switchroom

R5

3-Position switchboard

R10   R13   R12

Battery room

R6

WCs

Blast wall

Entrance 3

R14

Entrance 2

Redrawn from an original survey by Nick Catford

Entrance 1

Above: A view from R8, the Night Warden's room, through room R9 towards R 10 and entrance No.1.

Below: The remains of the ventilation fan in plant room R1.

Below right: The derelict carcass of the three-position telephone switchboard.

Above: A view from room R3, looking north through the main control room towards the ventilation plant room in the background.

Orpington

The Southern Railway's South East Division emergency control centre is located at the rear of the former engine shed on the eastern side of the railway station. Of the two original entrances the one easily visible to public view beside a footpath running beneath the railway line has been securely blocked. The main entrance, on Network Rail property at the rear of the old engine shed is protected by a brick blast-wall and has a light concrete canopy above the steel entrance door. The principal accommodation consists of two large rooms, an interconnecting corridor, air-locks at each entrance and a small room which contained ventilation and electrical equipment.

Below: A wooden rifle-rack, for local defence weapons, behind the inner gas-lock door at Orpington.

Above: The prominent concrete canopy over the main entrance.

Below: The control room in the Orpington bunker. The legend on the detached gas-lock door reads 'Air Lock - Upon receipt of the purple or red gas warning close all steel doors when entering or leaving the shelter. The first door must be closed before opening the second'.

Redhill

The South Central Divisional emergency control centre lies below a prominent earth mound to the south of the old goods shed at the rear of the car park at Redhill station. The bunker is surmounted by a more recent single-storey red-brick building housing telephone switching equipment, and is easily identifiable by the prominent, tall tapered concrete ventilation shaft that protrudes from its roof. Similar in design to the Orpington bunker, but without the external blast walls and canopy, the Redhill bunker remained operational until the mid-1960s. It, and the former telephone exchange building standing on its roof, have been converted into office accommodation for local permanent-way maintenance staff.

Woking

The South Eastern Divisional emergency control bunker at Woking is similar in design to that at Orpington but with a more substantial blast wall and canopy protecting its main entrance.

Below: The Woking bunker stands in the corner of the car park at Woking station.

Above: The entrance to the Redhill bunker.
Below: The ventilation plant room in the Redhill bunker. A dilapidated wood-cased railway telephone lies on the trunking in the right foreground.

Chapter 9

LOCAL AUTHORITY BUNKERS

When the Cold War ended in 1992 responsibility for most of the measures intended to ensure the health, welfare and ultimate survival of the population, and for the continuity of the nation's social structure in the aftermath of a nuclear war, had devolved upon Britain's local authorities; the County, District and Borough Councils. Following a brief period of euphoria at the end of the Second World War, it soon became apparent that the ideological tensions between the Soviet Union and the United States of America might once again lead to war in Europe. With this came the consequent risk of an atomic attack on the United Kingdom which had become, in the words of the investigative journalist Duncan Campbell, America's unsinkable aircraft carrier. As a precautionary measure the Civil Defence Corps, which had been wound-up at the end of the war, was re-established in 1948 under local authority control to operate in its old, wartime role of rescue and recovery. With the advent, by the 1950s, of ballistic missiles carrying nuclear warheads of hitherto unimaginable destructive power, however, the old concepts of rescue and recovery were seen increasingly as anachronistic and irrelevant. The scale of destruction would be so catastrophic that great swathes of Britain's population, her industrial base and social institutions would be wiped out, and that society would survive, at best, at a minimal level of subsistence. It was realised, too, that the post-war struggle for survival and subsequent period of recovery might last for years or even decades. Thus, by the early 1960s, the life-saving role of the local authorities, through the medium of the volunteer Civil Defence force, evolved into a more formalised organisation structured to ensure the preservation of a framework of bureaucratic administration best suited to meet the aims of long-term economic reconstruction.

It was assumed that in the event of nuclear war, communications with central government would be so disrupted that, for the survival of the nation, administrative powers would be devolved to a regional level. In the early 1950s the country was divided administratively into fourteen regions, and each was provided with a hardened Regional War Room from which a government-appointed Regional Commissioner

Above: The Mill Hill Regional War Room in Partington Lane. Built in 1952 to control the northern group of London boroughs, it became redundant in 1958. In 2010 the bunker was redeveloped as a luxury residential property known as Seafield House.

would exercise most of the powers of central government. Below the Regional War Rooms in the emergency government hierarchy stood the local authorities who were instructed, by a Home Office memorandum issued in March 1952, to construct bomb-proof main and subordinate Civil Defence control centres. By the 1960s the Regional War Rooms were seen as no longer fit for purpose, being too poorly protected and too close to the centres of the cities most likely to be prime Soviet targets, and too small to house the extended staff required for the task of long-term post-war rehabilitation. Their function was usurped by a series of new, more comprehensively equipped Regional Seats of Government. Meanwhile, more and more of the day-to-day tasks of social administration were devolved upon the local authorities, and regular Home Office circulars instructed these authorities to produce ever more sophisticated plans

Above: Deep beneath this nondescript bungalow at Kelvedon Hatch lies a three-level bunker, built in 1953 as the Metropolitan Sector Operations Centre for RAF Fighter Command. Redundant by 1958, it later became the Regional Government Headquarters for the London region.

Below: Hidden by anonymity in Lambeth's Central Hill Estate, Pear Tree House concealed the emergency control centre for South East London. The bunker is accessed via a blast door near the bottom of the upper flight of steps.

ORGANISATION OF THE LONDON GROUP & BOROUGH CONTROL CENTRES

North Western Group	Northern Group	North Eastern Group
Headquarters at Southall Civil Defence Control	Headquarters at Mill Hill War Room	Headquarters at Wanstead War Room
Harrow Brent Kensington & Chelsea Hammersmith & Fulham Hounslow Ealing Hillingdon	Barnet Camden City of London Enfield Harringey Islington Westminster	Wanstead Barking & Dagenham Hewham Tower Hamlets Hackney Waltham Forest Redbridge

South Western Group		South Eastern Group	
Headquarters at Cheam War Room		Headquarters initially at Chislehurst War Room, later at Pear Tree House in Lambeth	
Wansworth Lambeth Merton Sutton Kingston upon Thames Richmond on Thames		Greenwich Bexley Bromley Croydon Lewisham Southwark	

for the management of essential services in their counties or county boroughs in time of war. The Home Office instructions were enacted with varying degrees of enthusiasm, depending largely upon the political persuasion of the local authority concerned and, despite the availability of substantial central government grants offered in the mid-1980s, many counties and boroughs paid little more than lip service to the demands made upon them. The consequence of this is that in some authorities there exist modern, well equipped and sophisticated underground emergency centres, while at others there are to be found direly inadequate, half-heartedly adapted former Civil Defence control centres dating from the immediate post-war period.

Initially, the London boroughs were divided into five Groups, each of which was to be provided with a War Room similar to, but somewhat smaller than, the provincial Regional War Rooms. Only four of the five War Rooms were completed, however, and the North West Group was administered from an adapted former Civil Defence control centre at Southall. Following the reorientation of emergency war planning in the early 1960s, the London War Rooms were retained but they became Group Controls reporting to one of the new Regional Seats of Government, established in a three-level underground bunker at Kelvedon Hatch in Essex that was formerly the Metropolitan Sector Operations Room for the short-lived *ROTOR* air-defence radar system.

Above: The Bexley Borough Control was built beneath open ground on the Broadway, Bexleyheath, in 1953. When the new Bexley Civic Centre was built on the same site some years later, the entrance to the bunker was retained within a courtyard in the middle of the Civic Centre complex. The glazed stairway seen above leads down to a steel blast-door that gives access to the underground control centre.

Bexley

Right: The sick bay or medical centre in the Bexley Borough control centre. The small but massively constructed blast-door in the centre of the picture secures an emergency exit, consisting of a thirty-feet-long horizontal concrete pipe terminating in a vertical shaft containing a ladder up to a manhole in the courtyard above.

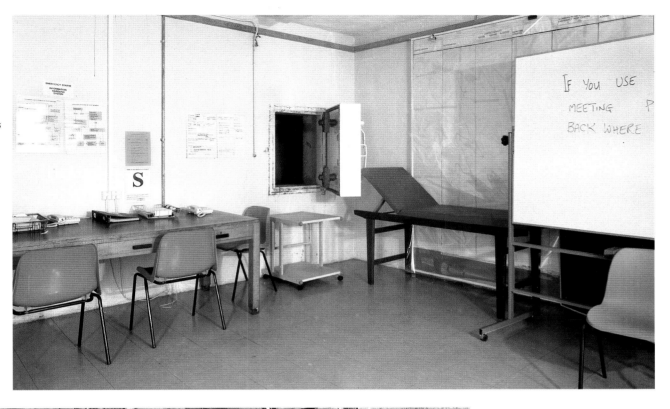

Camden

Left: Accessed via a rectangular concrete blockhouse located in a public park near the junction of Highgate Road and Gordon House Road, the Camden Emergency Centre was built in 1953 and abandoned in 1968. This view shows the central control room and Scientific Advisor's room in the Camden bunker, which has deteriorated badly due to the ingress of moisture. Note the short steel ladder leading to the emergency escape hatch.

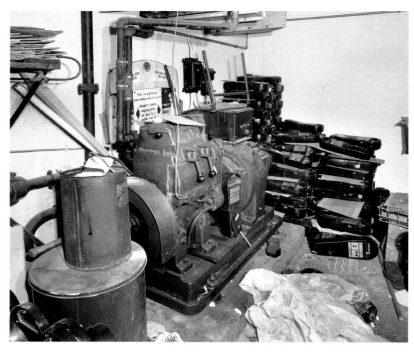

Chelsea

Above left: Chelsea Borough Control was built beneath the car park behind Chelsea Old Town Hall in 1954 and remained in use until the merger of Chelsea and Kensington Councils in 1964.

Above right: The original Chelsea bunker is now used by the Borough Highways Department as a workshop for the maintenance of parking meters. The standby generator is part of the original 1950s installation.

Dagenham

Left: The control room of the Dagenham Borough Emergency Centre, located at the rear of the Civic Centre at the junction of Wood Lane and Rainham Road North. Access is gained via a blast-door in a sloping-roofed blockhouse typical of other similar structures built in the 1950s. The bunker was decommissioned in 1968 with the winding-up of the Civil Defence Corps, but briefly reinstated during the period of extraordinarily cold winters in the 1990s.

East Ham

Above left: The entrance blockhouse for East Ham Borough Control. Built in the middle of Manor Park in 1953, the bunker was decommissioned in 1965 when the borough was amalgamated with West Ham. The bunker has now been infilled and the entrance demolished.

Edmonton

Above Right: The entrance to Edmonton's Borough Control, built in 1958 in the basement of the Plevna Road Clinic. The bunker was placed under care and maintenance in 1968. When Emergency Planning was revitalised in the 1980s, however, the council decided to establish a new control centre beneath Enfield Town Hall.

Right: Edmonton Borough Council considered plans to re-activate the Plevna Road control centre in 1990 but discovered that the basement was flooded to a depth of three feet. The cost of pumping and waterproofing the site was deemed too expensive and the plan was abandoned. The building was demolished in 2008 and the site is now occupied by a supermarket.

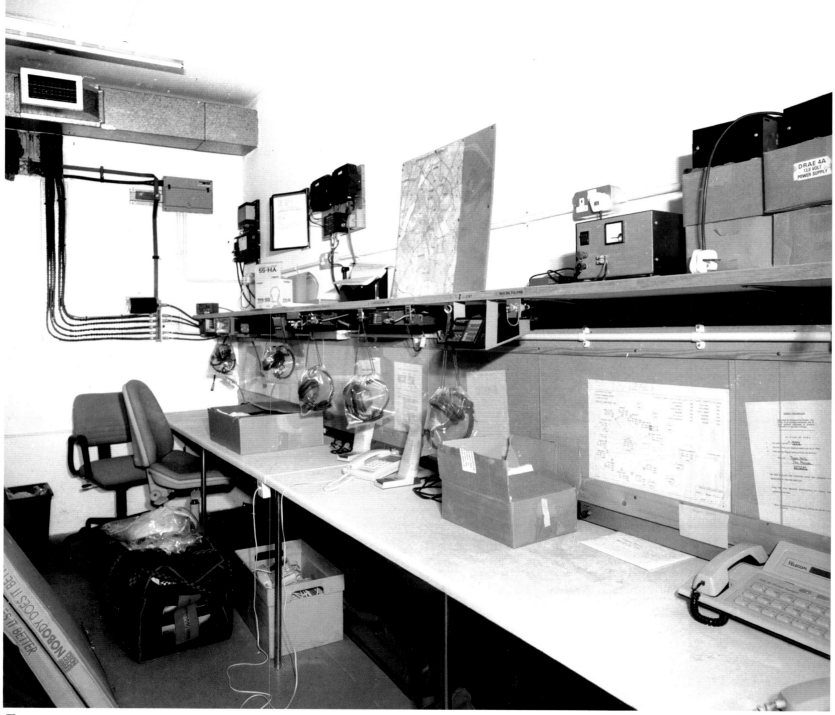

Epsom   *Above:* The Epsom Borough Emergency Centre was located in the basement of the new extension to Town Hall in The Parade in Epsom. Before construction was completed the Cold War drew to an end and the bunker became an irrelevance. Although the main blast-doors had been fitted, most of the internal fixtures and fittings remained unfinished. The only completed area is the radio room, seen here, which remains available for use.

Finsbury

Left: A two-level Civil Defence Control Centre was built beneath Gamault Place, to the left of the Town Hall at Finsbury, in 1940. The control room was on the lower floor while the upper floor acted as an air-raid shelter for Town Hall employees. The bunker was used for storage after the war until re-activated in 1952 to serve a similar role during the Cold War. In 1959 it was reduced to a Sub-Area Control beneath an Area Control located in a similar Second World War bunker in Islington. The Boroughs of Finsbury and Islington combined in 1965, when the Finsbury bunker was demoted to a Sector Post. It was placed under care and maintenance in 1968 and subsequently abandoned by the left-wing council.

Below left: The messengers' room on the lower floor, before it was completely flooded. Note the gas-tight door at the bottom of the stairs.

Below right: The top of the stairway to the now-flooded lower floor.

Friern Barnet

Above: Friern Barnet Town Hall was built between 1939 and 1941 with the basement housing a purpose-built Civil Defence Control Centre. The bunker was reactivated in 1954 as the Barnet UDC Control, remaining in use until 1965 when the new Borough of Barnet was formed. Control then moved to the former WW2 decontamination station at Dawes Lane, Mill Hill. The bunker was demoted to a Sector Post, remaining in use until 1968. The main entrance is via a flight of stairs within the Town Hall, but there are also two emergency escape shafts, one of which is seen here, that emerge in the Town Hall car park.

Opposite: This manually operated air-filtration unit in the Friern Barnet bunker dates from the Second World War.

Haringey

Above right: In 1956 Wood Green UDC built an emergency centre beneath the north wing of its new Civic Centre. In 1965 Wood Green merged with Tottenham and the now redundant bunker was redesignated as the Haringey Borough Control Centre. It fell into disuse in 1968 but was reactivated in 1988 to serve as Haringey Borough Emergency Centre. The main access is from within the Civic Centre with an emergency exit, seen here, terminating beside the road nearby.

Below right: The communications room at Haringey with radio equipment on the desk in the background and, in the foreground, a British Telecom SX50 PABX in its Electro-Magnetic-Pulse-protected cabinet.

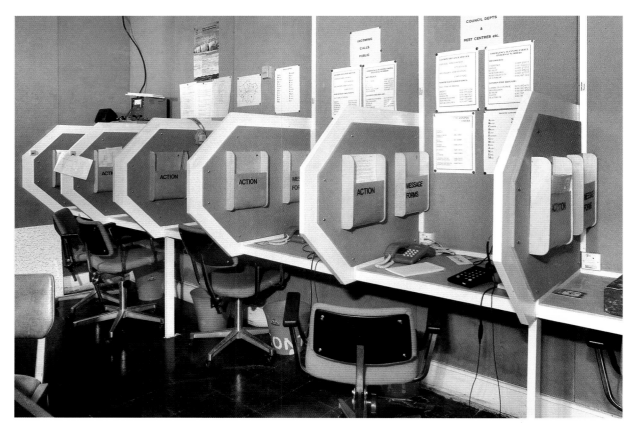

Hillingdon
Left: The communications room in the Hillingdon Emergency Centre, constructed beneath Uxbridge Civic Centre in the mid-1970s. Once much larger, at the end of the Cold War parts of the control centre were converted into the Civic Centre Sports and Social Club.

Paddington
Below left: The entrance to the Paddington Control Centre in the middle of a shrubery in Paddington Green. The bunker was abandoned and the entrance sealed many years ago.

Richmond
Below right: The Richmond Control Centre was constructed with the aid of a 100% government grant during the mid-1980s. It occupies the basement of Thames Link House on the corner of Church Road and Kew Road in Richmond and is still operational.

Southall

Right: The Southall Borough Control was originally constructed as a Civil Defence Control Centre during the Second World War and was enlarged to fulfil its Cold War role in the early 1960s. The bunker was constructed beneath an area of open land on South Road in Southall, but in 1983 Hambrough Primary School was built on top of it with one of its four entrances incorporated into the north side of the main school entrance. The centre was abandoned at about the time the school was built and it is probable that the problem of flooding, which is evident in this photograph, was caused by structural damage during the building of the school.

This view shows the main access corridor. The three vault doors are presumed to have secured the council's muniment rooms.

Left: The remains of the Southall tape relay centre with some of the sound-proof teleprinter housings and dial units still in place. This room, too, has been badly affected by the ingress of water.

Southwark

Above left: Southwark Borough Control was concealed beneath a health centre opposite the Town Hall, at the junction of Peckham Road and Vestry Road. The health centre was demolished in the 1990s and most of the stairwell leading to the bunker below filled in, leaving only a small access manhole protected by a steel grille.

Above right: The south end of the communications room showing four of the five acoustic booths, labelled 'SE Group Flood Net', 'Borough Net', 'Raynet', 'Tele Op.1' and 'Tele Op.2'. A glazed hatch at the end of the room communicates with the adjacent control room and is labelled 'Incoming Messages'.

Left: The opposite end of the communications room with the teleprinter room in the background.

Stoke Newington

Right: The entrance to the Stoke Newington Borough Control is a sloping concrete blockhouse similar to others built in the early 1950s. The bunker is at the rear of Stoke Newington Town Hall and is accessed from Lordship Terrace. In 1964 the Hackney Borough Control became unusable due to water ingress and it was briefly collocated at Stoke Newington. A year later, in 1965, the two boroughs merged and the Stoke Newington bunker was renamed Hackney Borough Control.

Left: The teleprinter room, with two Creed Type 7 teleprinters, enclosed in acoustic housings, together with power supplies and dialling units, still in place. In recent years the bunker has become a dumping ground for redundant computer equipment pending disposal.

Above: The standby generator at Stoke Newington, still in remarkably good condition.

Tottenham

Above left: The Tottenham Borough Control was built beneath a former council depot behind Tottenham Town Hall, which had seen little use for decades and was closed completely in 1990. The whole site was redeveloped in 2003. The bunker was built in 1954 and was abandoned in 1968 following the stand-down of the Civil Defence Corps. The entrance blockhouse, of a similar sloping design to those found in other London boroughs, was demolished when the site was cleared in the 1990s and the entrance stairwell sealed with concrete. In 2001 the underground research group Subterranea Britannica obtained permission to re-open the bunker to record and photograph its contents.

Above: The spine corridor running through the centre of the bunker.

Left: Most of the fixtures, fittings and service equipment had been removed after closure except for the ventilation plant, seen here.

Chapter 10

ROYAL OBSERVER CORPS MONITORING POSTS

The Royal Observer Corps was a volunteer organisation that watched the skies over Britain from often remote and isolated observation posts during the Second World War, searching for enemy aircraft and reporting back via Group and Sector Headquarters to the Air Defence Control Room at RAF Bentley Priory. This information, supplemented by data from the fledgling radar system, enabled Fighter Command and Anti-Aircraft Command to co-ordinate the air defence of the United Kingdom.

Following the end of the war in Europe, the Royal Observer Corps was stood down in May 1945, only to be re-formed in January 1947 as the threat of war with the Soviet Union clouded the skies over Britain. By the early 1950s the advent of, first, high-speed, high-altitude jet bombers carrying atomic bombs, and then of nuclear-tipped inter-continental ballistic missiles, rendered the Royal Observer Corps in its current form redundant.

Whilst it was accepted that there was no defence against ballistic missiles, successive governments understood that millions of lives might be saved, away from the impact zones, if there was adequate warning and time to take shelter. In 1963 the commissioning of the ballistic missile early-warning radar station on Fylingdales Moor in Yorkshire, capable of detecting the launch of Soviet missiles over the horizon and thousands of miles away, provided the now infamous 'four-minute warning', and with it a slim chance of survival. This chance of survival would be much enhanced if the power and location of nuclear impacts could be determined and the track of the ensuing radioactive fallout clouds accurately predicted. In 1955 the United Kingdom Warning and Monitoring Organisation, (UKWMO), was established to collect and collate such information and distribute it to the local authorities (who were ultimately responsible for civil protection), to a number of government and armed-forces headquarters, and to Britain's NATO partners. The Royal Observer Corps was to become the eyes and ears of this new organisation.

To facilitate this, over 1,500 blast and radiation protected, three-person underground monitoring posts were built during the 1950s and 1960s. This huge building programme resulted in a network of such posts located approximately eight miles apart on a grid that covered the entire country. Provided with simple, reliable and robust instruments, and reporting back through Group and Sector Control bunkers, the posts could warn the public and provide accurate data regarding the intensity of a nuclear attack and the subsequent spread of radioactive fallout.

Following the end of the Cold War, the organisation was disbanded in 1991 and the underground monitoring posts were abandoned. Seventeen such posts were constructed within the M25 boundary, of which ten have been completely and two partially demolished.

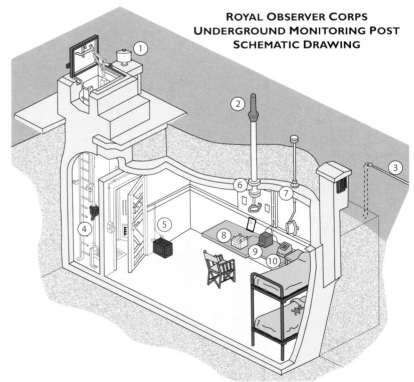

**ROYAL OBSERVER CORPS
UNDERGROUND MONITORING POST
SCHEMATIC DRAWING**

1	Ground Zero Indicator	6	Telescopic Probe Rod
2	FSM dome cover	7	Bomb Power Indicator
3	GPO line	8	Fixed Survey Meter
4	Sump pump	9	AD3460 Teletalk
5	Battery	10	WB400

Above: The Master ROC Post at RAF Northolt lies just twenty yards from the airfield control tower.

Above: The ROC Post at Hounslow is airside at Heathrow airport which made gaining permission to photograph it very difficult.

Above: The monitoring room at the Elstree ROC Post shortly before closure.

Above: The overgrown surface features of the long-abandoned New Malden Post, hidden in undergrowth on the edge of Malden golf course.

Above: The crew of the Colindale Post pose by the entrance hatch on the last day of operation in 1968. The post has been demolished.

Above and opposite: Interior views of the restored ROC Post at Knockolt. Through the door in the image above can be seen the drainage sump and pump at the base of the access shaft. The photograph opposite shows various post instruments, including an orange PDRM82 radiation monitor, a blue and yellow AD8010 Teletalk and, mounted on the wall above, a bomb-power indicator.

Above: After closure, the post at Enfield in Middlesex was demolished and the ground levelled, leaving little evidence of its existence. In July 2000 the landowner excavated the site with a mechanical digger to reveal that the concrete roof had been smashed and the monitoring room filled with rubble.

Above: The ROC Post at Dulwich stands on the edge of a golf course and has been converted into a small underground reservoir.
Below: Located on a hilltop south of the Esher bypass, the Oxshott Post has been heavily graffitied but many of the larger features have survived.

Above: Chigwell ROC Post, located near Roding Lane on the north side of RAF Chigwell. Since this photograph was taken in the Spring of 1997 the entrance shaft has been sealed with concrete.
Below: The vandalised interior of the Chigwell Post.

Chapter 11

GPO UNDERGROUND RAILWAY

In the early years of the twentieth century the GPO was looking for a more economic and expeditious way of transferring letters and parcels between its principal sorting offices and reception and distribution centres in London; the process having become hopelessly inefficient by conventional means as the streets of central London grew increasingly congested. The sub-surface geology of London made the concept of an underground railway both practical and economic, as had been demonstrated by the rapid development of underground passenger services in the capital in recent years. In 1909 a GPO committee recommended that a six-mile-long, twin-track, two-foot-gauge railway should be constructed in tunnels seventy feet below ground linking the Paddington District Office in the west to the Eastern District Office at Whitechapel Road in the east. Six intermediate stations were to be constructed at the Western Parcels Office in Barrett Street, the Western District Office in Wimpole Street, West Central District Office in New Oxford Street, Mount Pleasant Sorting Office, King Edward Building in King Edward Street and the Great Eastern Railway station at Liverpool Street.

Parliamentary approval was granted in 1913 and an experimental length of tunnel was constructed during the following year. The tests having proved successful a contract was awarded to John Mowlem, a firm with an impressive pedigree which in more recent years was responsible for construction of the Docklands Light Railway and London City Airport amongst a plethora of other major civil engineering projects. The tunnelling task, using Greathead shields, was completed towards the end of 1917 at which point work was suspended due to the wartime shortages of labourers and materials. In response to the threat of bombing posed by German Zeppelins, the almost completed station at King Edward Building was used as a safe repository for pictures from the Tate Gallery and National Portrait Gallery, and artefacts from the Public Records Office. Pictures from the Royal Collection and items from the Wallace Collection in Manchester Square were stored in the Post Office underground station at Paddington.

Construction resumed in 1920 and the first completed section, from Paddington to the West Central District office, entered service carrying parcel traffic on 24 January 1927. The next section of line, to Mount Pleasant sorting office, came into use on 3 December 1927,

GENERAL POST OFFICE
UNDERGROUND RAILWAY

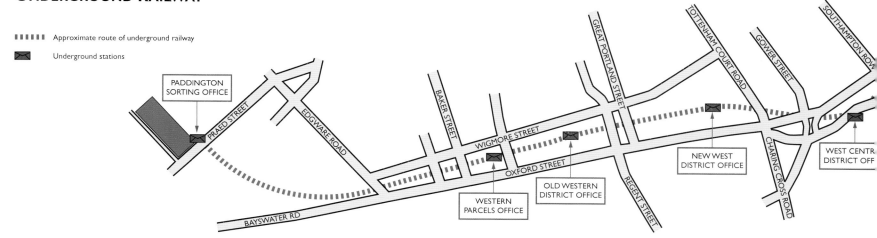

just in time to handle the Christmas rush. The final section, from Liverpool Street to the Eastern District Office in Whitechapel, was opened in January 1928. Initially the railway handled only parcel traffic; letters were not carried until 13 February 1929.

Between stations, the twin track rails were carried in a single, nine-foot-diameter segmented iron tube but on the approach they separated into independent seven-foot tubes before entering the twenty-five-feet-diameter station tunnels. The stations consisted of island platforms between the running lines with loop lines to carry through-traffic. The trains were unmanned and were initially controlled by a combined system of automatic stops and local control from signal cabins at each station. In 1993 all train handling was transferred to an automatic, computerised central control located at Mount Pleasant, although the local signal cabins were retained for emergency use. Trains travelled at seven miles per hour. The lines at each end of the stations were on a rising incline of 1:20 in order that trains approaching would be slowed down as they drew into the stations and departing trains would be accelerated on exit.

Over the years many extensions to the system were proposed but none was ever implemented. A deviation to the line was made, however, in 1958 when the Western District Office was relocated to Rathbone Place. This scheme was first considered in 1954 but nothing was done until 1958, with the new deviation finally coming

into use on 3 August 1963. The original tunnel was retained for use as storage.

The original rolling stock, built by English Electric and introduced in 1927, consisted of ninety, four-wheeled units used in trains of three. These were under-powered and unreliable and were replaced by two new batches of power units in 1930 and 1936 utilising much of the electrical equipment of the original stock. These were more satisfactory and it was not until 1962 that the next new vehicles were acquired. These consisted of just two units, the first of which was withdrawn after just five years. The second was withdrawn in 1980 but re-entered service using parts cannibalised from its sister and survived until 2003. The 1930s stock was largely replaced in the early 1980s by thirty-four new units purchased from Hunslet of Leeds.

The line operated with reasonable efficiency until the latter years of the twentieth century, but in November 2002 it was announced that it had been running at an unsustainable loss for several years. At that time the Royal Mail was losing a staggering £1,200,000 per day, and any potential economy measure was welcomed. In the face of much popular opposition, the line was finally closed on 3 May 2003 and in now lies disused and abandoned but still largely intact beneath the city streets.

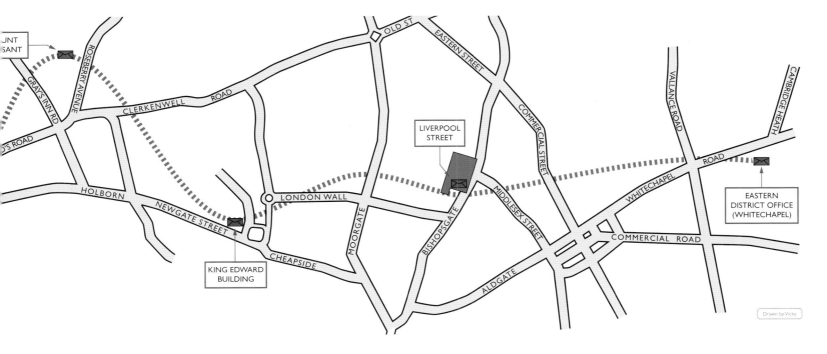

Above: A mail train emerges from the tunnel into the westbound platform at Mount Pleasant station while an empty eastbound train waits on the through line.

Opposite: One of the thirty-four power units ordered from Greenwood & Batley of Leeds in 1980. The company went into receivership in April 1980 after only three units were completed, but the business was purchased by Hunslet Holdings Ltd, also of Leeds, who completed the order. Hunslet continued to use the Greenbat name on all the battery electric locomotives it manufactured.

Above: One of the four English Electric battery locomotives used on the Post Office railway for maintenance purposes and for the recovery of broken-down trains.

Opposite: The manual slide-lever interlocking frame in the signal-box at Mount Pleasant station. Although signalling and train control on the Post Office railway was transferred to a central computerised system in 1933, signal-boxes like this at each station could take local control in an emergency.

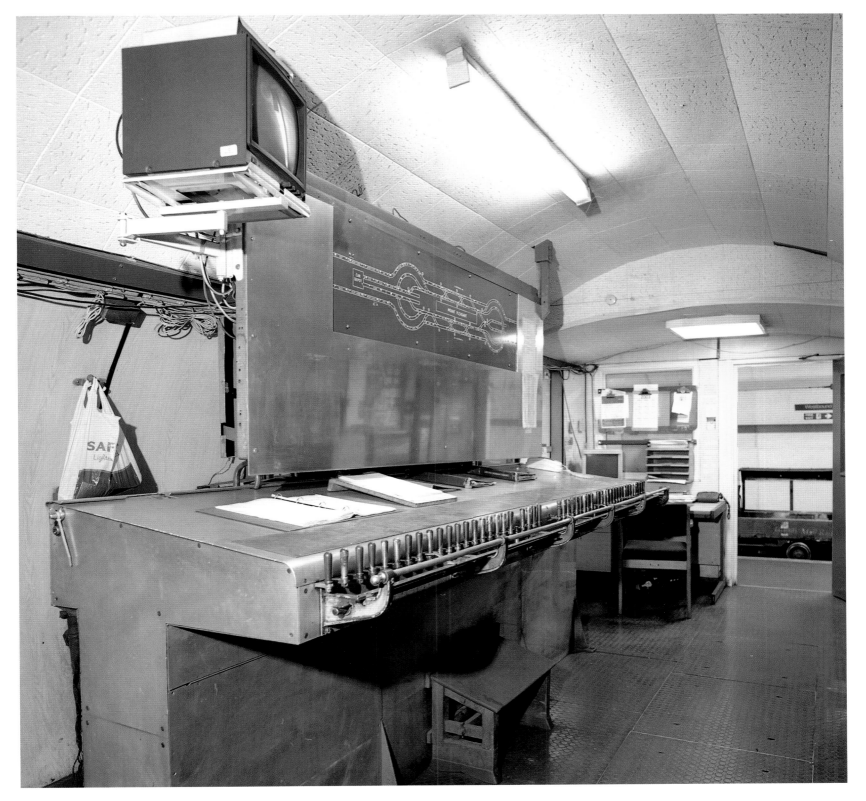

Above: The new control room at Mount Pleasant from where, after 1993, all train movements were co-ordinated. Note the track diagrams for each station above the controller's console. The monitors on the right-hand side gave the train controllers a real-time view of what was happening on the platforms and in the tunnels via closed-circuit television links.

Chapter 12

BISHOPSGATE GOODS STATION

Above: The derelict remains of one of the three hydraulic lifts which raised and lowered wagons between the surface and the underground goods yard. This was once surrounded by a maze of sidings, all of which were lifted in 1967.

Bishopsgate started life as the City terminus of the Eastern Counties Railway, opening in July 1840. A year later, in July 1841, the London & Blackwall Railway, which later was incorporated into the London, Tilbury & Southend Railway, opened its terminus at Fenchurch Street; this it shared, from 1850 to 1865, with the North London Railway until the latter company built its own terminus at Broad Street. In 1862 the Eastern Counties Railway amalgamated with a number of smaller railway companies in East Anglia to form the Great Eastern Railway. Suburban traffic on the Great Eastern soon increased beyond the capacity of the inconveniently positioned Bishopsgate terminus and under an agreement with the London Tilbury & Southend Railway some Great Eastern trains ran into Fenchurch Street. However, this arrangement was still not sufficient and, having failed in 1864 to gain Parliamentary consent for a terminal station in the West End, the Great Eastern opted instead to build a new terminus at Liverpool Street, which was fully opened for all traffic on 1 November 1875.

The opening of Liverpool Street rendered Bishopsgate redundant as a passenger station and by 1881 it had been rebuilt and extended to form a very extensive goods station handling most of the freight traffic to and from the whole of eastern England. The original Eastern Counties line ran into Bishopsgate on a long viaduct designed by John Braithwaite, one of the earliest of its kind and, in terms of architectural history, one of the most important on the British railway system. As Bishopsgate goods yard extended, the western end of Braithwaite's viaduct became incorporated within its structure.

The yard was on three levels with the main line entering and fanning out into an array of sidings at viaduct level. Above main-line level was a vast warehouse while below, down amongst the vaults and arches that supported the main line and sidings, was a further network of standard-gauge sidings interlinked by wagon turntables and with motive power provided by hydraulic capstans. There was no direct rail connection to the lower-level sidings, instead, wagons were interchanged between levels by means of three hydraulic wagon lifts powered by massive, weight-driven hydraulic accumulators.

In December 1964 the upper-floor warehouse at Bishopsgate was completely destroyed by a spectacular fire and within a few years the entire site was an overgrown, weed-strewn ruin with parts used by squatters and others used for car parking. Plans for the extension of London Transport's East London Line, proposed in 1989, threatened what remained of the goods yard and the Braithwaite viaduct. There was much local and national opposition, English Heritage expressed apprehension over the future of the viaduct and so much concern was generated that a public enquiry was called for. Meanwhile, the lower level of the former goods yard had been converted by Bishopsgate Space Management Ltd into a mixed leisure, commercial and residential development. The long-running enquiry eventually decided that the demolition should go ahead, with caveats safeguarding part of the Braithwaite viaduct, and in May 2002 Bishopsgate Space Management's tenants were served with eviction notices. In 2003 demolition started in order to make way for the East London Line's Shoreditch High Street station.

Above: The lower rail level at Bishopsgate in 1995. A turntable pit for one of the transverse lines can be seen in the right foreground. In the background, daylight streams through the aperture of the wagon hoist illustrated on the previous page.

Opposite: One of the depot's two hydraulic accumulators. The scale of the cylinder may be judged from the size of the discarded pallets dumped around it. When in use, fifty tons of iron weights would have been suspended from the piston crosshead.

Above: Discovered in a basement store-room, these decaying shelves contain Great Eastern Railway personnel files, some dating back to 1915.

Below: The position of the two turntables serving transverse lines which ran the full width of the western end of the lower rail level.

Above: These distinctive pointed arches in the office area on the lower rail level, between Shoreditch High Street and Wheeler Street, are similar to those found on the Braithwaite Viaduct.

Below: This attractive glazed wooden office was situated near the outer roadway of the lower rail level between Wheeler Street and Brick Lane.

Above: A view through the arches across the transverse line platforms on the lower rail level.

Above: A general view of the lower rail level at Bishopsgate Goods Station, showing the shallow brick arches
on the longitudinal platforms and the vaulted brick arches between the girders supporting the floor above.

Chapter 13

SNOW HILL STATION

SNOW HILL STATION & CONNECTIONS

- ● Open station
- ● Closed station
- ■ Closed goods depot

Redrawn from an original survey by Nick Catford

Above: The south portal of Snow Hill tunnel in 1985, fourteen years after the rails were lifted. A year after this photograph was taken, in December 1986, the rails were reinstated as part of the Thameslink project.

The Metropolitan Extension Act of 1860 gave the London Chatham and Dover Railway access to the City via a four-and-a-half-mile-long line from Herne Hill crossing the Thames to join the Metropolitan Railway at Farringdon Street. The line was too costly to construct by the financially hard-pressed LC&DR alone, but was of great financial and strategic significance as a cross-London link. It was of particular significance to the railway companies in southeast England who could access the line via Clapham Junction, and to the Great Northern Railway and Midland Railway to the north, with which the new line would make direct contact. Direct connection could also be made to the Great Western and the London and North Western Railways which could be reached via the West London Line. All the companies became financially involved in return for running powers,

the lines from the north benefiting particularly by gaining the right to establish their own coal yards in South London.

The first section of line, from Herne Hill to Elephant and Castle, was opened in October 1862. The line was extended over the Thames in 1864 and the first LC&DR trains ran into Farringdon Street via Blackfriars and Ludgate Hill on 1 January 1866. By this time the London Chatham and Dover Railway was bankrupt and unable to raise capital on its own account, but through the medium of a nominally independent company was able, in March 1874, to open a short branch to its own terminus at Holborn Viaduct. A few months later, in August 1874 a low-level station on the through-line to Farringdon was opened. Initially known as Snow Hill the station, enclosed in a tunnel at the foot of a sharp 1:39 incline, was renamed

Holborn Viaduct Low Level in 1912. Meanwhile, in September 1871, a new east-facing spur, known as the Smithfield Curve, had been constructed from just north of Snow Hill to Moorgate via Barbican.

For the first thirty years the new line carried heavy passenger traffic into the City but by the start of the First World War this was in serious decline, due principally to competition from the Northern Line tube. As a wartime economy measure, passenger traffic on the Smithfield Curve into Moorgate ceased in April 1916 and a few stations south of the Thames were closed. Then, in June 1916, Holborn Viaduct Low Level (Snow Hill) station closed and with it through passenger traffic on the City line ceased. The line remained an important north-south freight route, however, and as late as 1962 more than ninety trains a day passed over it. Freight and parcels traffic were finally withdrawn in 1969 and the rails through Snow Hill tunnel were lifted in 1971.

The tunnel achieved a new lease of life in 1988 when it was re-opened as part of the Thameslink network, which came into service in May 1990. During the reconstruction, Holborn Viaduct station was closed and the rails approaching it over Ludgate Hill removed. A new line was constructed dropping down steeply from Blackfriars to a new low-level station known as City Thameslink, built beneath the former Holborn Viaduct station.

Above: The Great Northern Railway's Farringdon Street goods depot. This photograph was taken in April 1981, but except for the fluorescent strip lights it could be almost timeless. The large double-doors in the background are lettered 'Corporation of London Salt Store. No Admittance'.

Opposite: The derelict remains of Holborn Low Level station in April 1985.

Chapter 14

CRYSTAL PALACE SUBWAY

Paxton's great Crystal Palace was erected in Hyde Park as a temporary structure to house the Great Exhibition of 1851 and was to have remained open for only six months from May to October. So great was its success, however, that it was decided that it should be dismantled and re-erected at a new site on Penge Common next to Sydenham Hill. The reconstructed Palace was opened by Queen Victoria in June 1854 as a tourist attraction and as a home for the Crystal Palace School of Art, Science and Literature and the Crystal Palace School of Engineering.

At first, the only train service to the new site was via the LB&SCR's inconveniently situated Low Level station in Anerley Road, which necessitated a long walk to the Palace, albeit beneath a glazed colonnade. To alleviate the problem a line was opened in August 1865 from Peckham Rye to a new Crystal Palace High Level Station, built by the Crystal Palace & South London Junction Railway Company. Access from the High Level station to the Palace was via a spectacular, vaulted and tiled subway beneath Crystal Palace Parade, designed in a Byzantine style by the architect Edward Middleton Barry. From the main floor of the Crystal Palace steps led down to a glazed concourse giving access to the station booking halls and the underpass.

Even by the time of the opening of the new station, however, public interest in the Crystal Palace was waning and by the 1890s the site had drifted down-market. The proprietors were declared bankrupt in

Opposite: The ornate vaulted and tiled ceiling of the Crystal Palace subway. Italian craftsmen expert in such work were brought across to complete the work.

Left: Steps once led down from the main floor of the Crystal Palace into this concourse which gave access via the four arched openings to the subway beneath Crystal Palace Parade and the two ticket halls at the High Level Station. A glazed canopy originally covered the subway concourse but this was destroyed when the Crystal Palace burned down in 1936.

1911 and thereafter the future of the Crystal Palace appeared bleak. The end came in November 1936 when the structure was completely destroyed by fire. Meanwhile, traffic on the new line continued to decline and services were gradually withdrawn. The line was closed in May 1944 as a wartime economy measure but reopened in January 1946. During the war the area suffered badly from enemy bombing and the subway was used as an air-raid shelter. Wartime damage to the station roof had never been repaired and the weather was taking its toll. The station was finally closed on 18 September 1954 and demolished in 1961, leaving only a high retaining wall on the west side of Crystal Palace Parade and the now roofless subway concourse as evidence of its existence.

Chapter 15

WATERLOO STATION TUNNELS

When the London and South Western Railway extended their line from the original terminus at Nine Elms to Waterloo in 1848, the approach to the new terminus, as well as the station itself, was constructed on brick arches to raise it above the marshy ground upon which it was built. As the station was extended through the latter part of the nineteenth century the arched undercroft became an ever more complex labyrinth of arched and vaulted chambers, tunnels and passageways. When the hopelessly ramshackle terminus was reconstructed in 1922 most of the original supporting arches were retained and, indeed, considerably extended.

Over time, all manner of uses were found for the tunnels, including the receipt, storage and despatch of parcels and light goods traffic and the transfer of parcels traffic between platforms. During the 1970s the Waterloo depot of British Rail's ill-fated Red Star parcels service was located there. The tunnels were also home to the wages-staff canteen and the bill store, which distributed pictorial posters to all Southern Region stations. Also located in the undercroft was the office of the Southern Region Telecommunications Engineer together with a telecoms workshop and stores. A further area, known as the 'plan arch', was a repository used by the Chief Civil Engineer's department for the storage of engineering and architectural drawings of bridges, stations and other railway structures. Up until the 1950s the railway's Waterloo telephone exchange was located beneath the arches, after which it was moved to the south side of the cab road above Lower Marsh. Nearby was the ambulance, or first aid, room which was subsequently occupied by the Waterloo staff Model Railway Club.

During the latter part of the nineteenth century parts of the tunnel complex were put to a more sombre use by the London Necropolis Company. To alleviate the problem of severe overcrowding in London's existing graveyards and cemeteries, the company established in 1854 a vast new cemetery at Brookwood in Surrey, some twenty-three miles from London. Coffins and mourners destined for the cemetery were carried over the company's own London Necropolis Railway, which had two stations within the cemetery grounds and a

London terminus at Waterloo, adjacent to the L&SWR station. The Necropolis Company's station was a building of some substance and included, as well as waiting rooms for mourners, the company offices, workshops and stores. An area of the vaults beneath the station was used as a mortuary and as a store for three hundred empty coffins. A mechanical lift raised the coffins from the vault to platform level. Some accounts describe it as a hydraulic lift, others as steam powered; given the spirit of the age it should have been the latter, even if it was not. During the expansion of Waterloo Station at the beginning

Below: Part of the maze of arched passageways beneath Waterloo Station.

Above: One of the many workshops and store-rooms beneath Waterloo Station. With the tasks previously performed there now out-sourced, these once busy workshops have become mere dumping grounds for redundant materials.

of the twentieth century the L&SWR financed the relocation of the Necropolis Company's station to a new site nearer to Waterloo Bridge Road. This was severely damaged by enemy bombing in April 1941 and never rebuilt although the entrance building was relatively unscathed and still stands today. No Necropolis trains ran after 1941 although coffins for Brookwood were carried in the guard's van of ordinary passenger trains for many years.

Currently, some of the vaults beneath the station remain in use as workshops or rough storage, and much use has been made of them as convenient pipe and cable routes. An area towards the southern end is now occupied by the Old Vic Theatre and used as performance and exhibition space.

Chapter 16

KINGSWAY TRAM TUNNEL

Above: The northern incline into the Kingsway Tram Tunnel, in the middle of Southampton Row. The rails visible in this photograph are the longest lengths of tram rail that survive in London.

The story of the Kingsway Tram Tunnel is one of astonishing managerial muddle and grand ambitions thwarted.

As part of the redevelopment of the run-down, slum-ridden Holborn area by the London County Council in the closing years of the nineteenth century, it was decided that a new tram line should be constructed from Theobalds Road to the Embankment at Waterloo Bridge. To ease traffic congestion, much of the route was to be built as a subway. As well as to ease traffic and transport in the immediate area, the County Council had a secondary motive for constructing the tram tunnel in that it would offer a convenient route, via a connection over Waterloo Bridge, between its northern lines and its principal maintenance workshop south of the Thames at Charlton.

Work began in 1902 but initially, due to legal obstacles concerning property leases, trams could run only to the north side of the Strand. These problems were eventually overcome in 1906 but in the interim the section of tunnel beyond Aldwych station, at which point public services terminated, had been fitted out as a repair and maintenance workshop. The eventual resolution of the legal difficulties that hampered completion of the tunnel did not mark the end of the Council's problems, however, for they were refused permission to extend their lines across Waterloo Bridge, which somewhat scuppered their scheme to provide a convenient link to the Charlton depot. Instead, the tunnel terminated with a new sharp curve beneath Lancaster Place leading to a surface exit through the western abutment of Waterloo Bridge where a junction was made with a new tramway then under construction on the Embankment. This new configuration rendered redundant the proposed tramway station at Wellington Street near the south end of the tunnel, for which Parliamentary approval had been granted in the 1905 session. A full public service on the through route was inaugurated on 24 February 1906.

Due to engineering difficulties posed by the presence just below the surface of the Holborn branch of the Fleet Sewer, and by the position of the sub-surface Metropolitan Railway at the Embankment, the inclines into and out of the tram subway were steeply graded and to cope with these it was decided, (somewhat unfortunately as it transpired), to work the line with single-deck trams. With limited headroom in the tunnel it was impossible to use the normal overhead current-collecting system so trams running in the tunnel had to do so using battery power. From Theobalds Road the tramway lines descended into a 170-foot-long open cutting in the middle of Southampton Row before entering a pair of cast-iron tubes, fourteen feet five inches in diameter, to pass beneath the Fleet Sewer at a depth of thirty-one feet below ground level. After 225 feet the lines rise at an incline of 1:10 and enter a twenty-foot-wide box-section tunnel just below road level. At this point the roof of the tunnel is supported by steel trough girders.

By the late 1920s it was apparent that the single-deck trams could never be operated profitably and it was decided that, despite the engineering obstacles, the Kingsway tunnel had to be enlarged to take double-deck trams although even these were still compelled to traverse the tunnel using battery power. Work started on the task of increasing headroom in the tunnel to sixteen feet six inches in September 1929 and was completed by 14 January 1931 when services were resumed. The cost had been in excess of £280,000, which included the rebuilding of fifty old single-deck trams with double-deck bodies. Further alterations were required in 1937 as a result of the rebuilding of Waterloo Bridge. The sharply curved tunnel leading to the exit portal in the west wall of the bridge abutment was abandoned and replaced by a straight length of tunnel that emerged onto the Embankment directly beneath the bridge.

June 1939 marked the beginning of the end for the Kingsway Tram Tunnel, for in that month the London County Council began running an experimental trolleybus. These vehicles would be quite unsuitable for operation in the tunnel. The wholesale replacement of tramcars by trolleybuses and motor buses was, however, delayed by the onset of the Second World War and the replacement programme did not begin until 1950. The last trams ran in London on 5 April 1952 and all the rails were lifted soon thereafter. The tracks in the now disused tunnel and on its approach incline at Southampton Row were left in situ and still remain today as the longest

Below: The north end of the tramway tunnel looking towards Holborn station. This section of tunnel was until recently used by Camden Council for the storage of road maintenance materials and redundant street furniture. A number of ornate, barley-twist lamp standards are stacked against the right-hand wall.

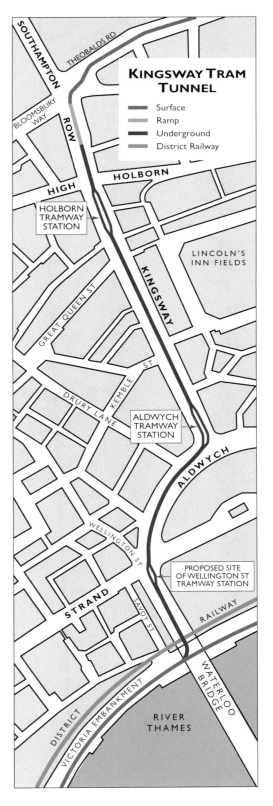

KINGSWAY TRAM TUNNEL

- Surface
- Ramp
- Underground
- District Railway

Above: Holborn station, showing one of the staircases leading to the surface.

surviving length of tramway in the capital.

Virtually unused, except for a brief period in the 1950s when a section was utilised for storage by an engineering company, the tunnel was forgotten about until 1958 when London County Council earmarked it as a possible solution to the problem of traffic congestion at the northern end of Waterloo Bridge. Construction of what was to become the Strand Underpass began in April 1962 and was completed in January 1964. A southern entrance ramp was constructed near Waterloo Bridge and an exit ramp near the junction of Kingsway and High Holborn at the site of the former Holborn tramway station. The northern section of the tunnel from Southampton Row to Holborn station remains largely untouched. The road underpass is built within the old tunnel, and at the site of Holborn station it is possible to see the underside of the ramp carrying the carriageway up to the surface. A narrow walkway between the original tunnel wall and the west wall of the Strand Underpass allows somewhat restricted access to surviving sections of the south end of the tunnel including the curve to the pre-1937 exit portal in the wing-wall of Waterloo Bridge. A short section of the new tunnel directly beneath the bridge has recently been transformed into a bar and restaurant.

In 1974 the Greater London Council Emergency Planning Department established a makeshift flood control centre in the Holborn tramway station at the time of their relocation from City Hall. Each of the London Boroughs had its own flood control centre which reported to the GLC central control at Holborn. The centre remained operational until 1984 when completion of the Thames Barrier rendered it redundant. In more recent years Camden Borough Council Highways Department has used parts of the tunnel for rough storage.

Below: From 1974 to 1984 this was the office of the Thames Flood Engineering Controller. It was subsequently used as rough storage for road maintenance equipment, but has now been removed.

Below: Noticeboards on the wall of the Flood Controller's office that once recorded the height of the tide at various locations on the Thames as far inland as Richmond Lock.

Above: The grey Portacabin in the background of this photograph of Holborn station, formerly the home of the Greater London Council Emergency Planning Department Flood Control Centre was until recently occupied by Camden Council Highways Department. It has now been removed.

Chapter 17

CAMDEN RAILWAY VAULTS & HORSE TUNNELS

Above: Wine barrels stored in Gilbey's vaults in Camden.

When the London and Birmingham Railway, forerunner of the London and North Western Railway, proposed an extension from its earlier terminus at Camden Town to a new location in Euston Grove, the company was faced with a formidable problem. The main line approached the new Euston terminus from London's northern heights via the steeply inclined Camden Bank and, from 1837 to 1844, a rope haulage system was employed to raise and lower trains up and down the bank, utilising a stationary winding engine at the top of the incline. This mode of propulsion was forced upon the railway company as a result of negotiations with the Dukes of Bedford and Southampton, who were keen to protect the value of their development land, particularly in Euston Square and Park Village East. They refused to allow any locomotive sheds or repair shops at Euston.

Parliamentary authorisation for the London and Birmingham Railway's extension to Euston, granted in 1835, compelled the company to cross the Regent's Canal allowing sufficient clearance for boats to pass unimpeded beneath. This necessitating the construction

of the railway some fifteen feet above the former ground level in the area in which Camden goods yard would later be established. Much of the land was built up to the requisite height using spoil, mainly blue London clay, excavated from Primrose Hill tunnel and its approach cutting. Part of the goods yard was later extended on vaults which were subsequently leased by the railway company for storage.

By the 1860s there had developed a network of interconnected, arched-roof vaults like a secret underworld beneath the area bounded by, and indeed extending beyond, Gloucester Avenue, the Regent's Canal and Chalk Farm Road, all of which was profitably employed. Meanwhile, vaults constructed beneath the top of the railway incline to house the engines and winding gear that drew trains up the bank were decommissioned in 1844 and the equipment removed. The vaults were sold by the railway company in 1847. To the northeast of the site, a series of vaults were built in 1846. By 1855 Allsopp's, like Bass, their bigger Burton rival, sent thousands of gallons of their beer weekly via the London and North Western Railway (which had absorbed the London and Birmingham in 1846), in order, one might think, to keep the working classes of London in a perpetual, happy state of inebriate quietude, but also because beer was a safer alternative to London's notoriously noxious water supplies. By 1866, these vaults were used by Bass and Samuel Allsopp & Sons, the second-largest brewer in Burton-on-Trent, as a beer store.

In 1855 the raised railway level was extended across land north of the Regent's Canal, allowing the LNWR to construct further vaults. An interchange dock ran through the vaults, facilitating the covered transfer of general merchandise from canal to rail and of beer and wine store from the various stores nearby. The L-shaped vaults southwest of the interchange docks, constructed in 1855, were initially leased to Allsopp's, but by 1866 at least 27,000 square feet were occupied by Bass and Company.

Some years later, in 1866, the London and North Western Railway built a large goods shed to the north of the canal, the basement beneath which was used to store general merchandise in transit. To the south of the canal, opposite the railway goods shed, the

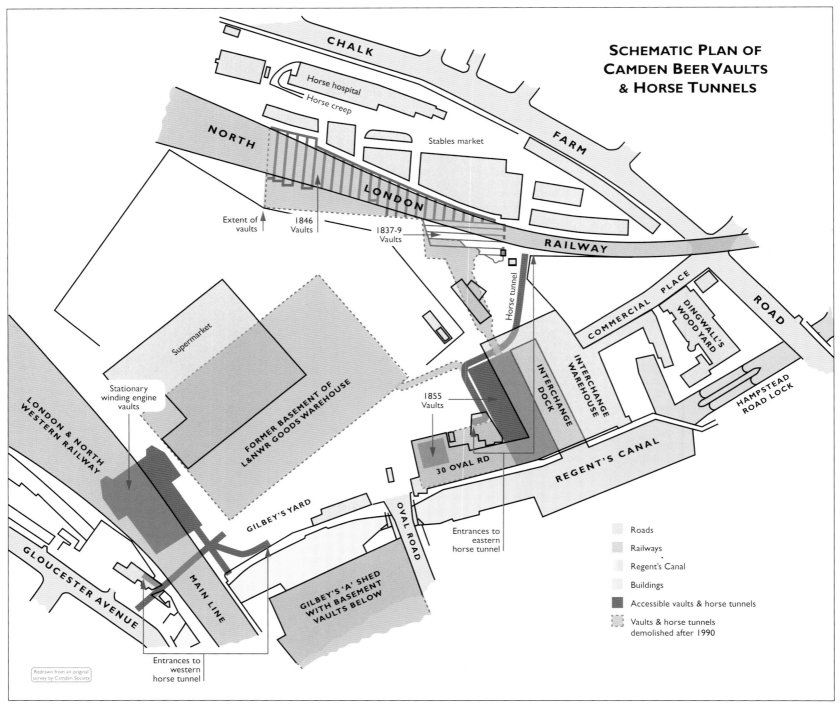

Above: A schematic diagram of the former Camden goods yard showing
the approximate disposition of the vaults and horse tunnels in relation to
contemporary surface features.

wine merchants W. & A. Gilbey converted, in 1869, a former Pickford warehouse, owned latterly by the LNWR, into an extensive wine store. Each floor of the warehouse extended over an area of two acres. The Gilbey brothers had generated a vast trade in non-vintage, inexpensive, but predictable and tolerably good wine. Later in the nineteenth century Gilbey's began production of their own dead-drunk-for-tuppence gin, and also produced their own whisky after buying a series of established Scottish distilleries. The vaults beneath the wine warehouse offered superb storage at a stable temperature for wines and spirits and eventually Gilbey's took over many of the existing vaults, previously leased by other merchants, to the north of the canal.

Throughout the nineteenth and early twentieth centuries horses provided the principal motive power for shunting movements within the railway yard and for the delivery and collection of merchandise. The London and North Western Railway owned an elaborate stable complex, with accommodation for 400 horses, fronting Chalk Farm Road, most of which was leased to other occupiers. Gilbey, Allsopp

and Pickford stabled almost as many again at other sites around the depot. To facilitate the safe movement of such large numbers of horses around the busy sidings, two horse tunnels were constructed running from the stables into the yards associated with the various warehouses. The western horse tunnel ran from stables west of the railway along Gloucester Avenue, under the main line and into Gilbey's yard, and into the basement beneath the goods shed. The eastern horse tunnel ran from the stables at the east end of the railway yard, beneath the sidings of Camden goods yard, and emerged at the west side of the interchange warehouse.

In recent years much of this underground infrastructure has been lost to development. Most of what remained of the 1839 vaults was demolished in 2007 to make way for the current Horse Tunnel Market, while the basement beneath the former goods shed was destroyed when the site was redeveloped as a supermarket. One arm of the L-shaped vaults of 1855 adjacent to the interchange dock was largely demolished in 2008 during the construction of Henson House.

Left: A view across the interchange basin towards the vaults beneath No.30 Oval Road.

Above: A section of the beer vaults adjacent to the interchange dock, looking northwest along the wall separating the vaults from the eastern horse tunnel.

Above: The southeast corner of the 1855 vaults close to where the interchange dock joins the Regent's Canal. The vaulted arches on the left gradually merge with the external wall of the building above, fronting the canal. Consisting of heavy timber baulks, the barrel-runs for Gilbey's wine casks are prominent in this picture. The foreground vault remains but everything else has been demolished.

Above: Vaulted sidings below the 1839 goods depot. The concrete path through the former sidings linked to Alsopp's (later Gilbey's) 1855 vaults under the forecourt of the interchange warehouse.

Above: Taken in 1988, this photograph and the one opposite, show sections of the eastern horse tunnel that had thus far avoided development or destruction. It is now in multi-ownership and has been blocked in more than one location. At the Stables Yard end, it is now a feature of Horse Tunnel Market.

Above: The basement of the former LNWR goods warehouse, showing part of the narrow-gauge railway system that served it. The warehouse was built in 1866 (the largest of its kind at that time), and was rebuilt in 1931. Shortly after this photograph was taken the warehouse was demolished and now forms the foundation of a supermarket and Gilbey's Yard social housing development.

Chapter 18

HYDRAULIC PIPE TUNNELS

Above: A typical hydraulic accumulator tower. This example is situated beside the former London Tilbury & Southend Railway where the line from Fenchurch Street crosses Mansell Street. The faded lettering reads 'London Midland & Scottish Railway City Goods Station and Bonded Stores'.

Prior to the outbreak of war in 1939 a vast, 180-mile web of hydraulic distribution pipes ran beneath the streets of London. These provided silent power to a staggering range of machinery including personnel and goods lifts in offices, warehouses and railway stations; presses and mills in factories; dockyard cranes and capstans; the opening gear for the stage curtains at the Royal Opera House and even the mechanism that raised and lowered the 700 ton central floor of the Earls Court Exhibition Centre. Many of the power mains were damaged by enemy action during the war and, due to the reduction in demand resulting from the post-war drift of industry away from the city centre, were not repaired or replaced. By 1950 the network had consequently contracted to approximately 150 miles but was to remain profitable, despite a diminishing customer base and

widespread electrification, for more than twenty years.

The London hydraulic system had its origins in the somewhat wordy Wharves and Warehousing Steam Power and Hydraulic Pressure Company, which was incorporated in 1871 to provide an alternative source of power for cranes, lifts and capstans in London's dockland. Centralised power, transmitted via high-pressure water, was seen to be much more economical and efficient compared with individual, small steam-powered units each with its own engine, boiler and ancillary plant. In 1884 the company was reconstituted as the more snappily named London Hydraulic Power Company and extended its customer base across the whole range of commercial, manufacturing and transport undertakings in the Capital. Over the years many large concerns, including the mainline and underground railway companies, which had earlier established their own local hydraulic power generation plants, chose to close them down and connect their machinery to the London Hydraulic Power Company's main instead.

Hydraulic power was produced at five main pumping stations located at Bessborough Gardens in Pimlico, Blackfriars Bridge, Albion Docks in Rotherhithe, Wapping Wall and at City Road in Islington. The total output of the five plants was approximately 7,000 horsepower. This power was propelled through the underground pipes at a pressure of 750 pounds per square inch. A reserve of energy was stored in accumulator towers which consisted of very large hydraulic rams surmounted by weights of up to 150 tons. Surplus power, when the demand on the system was less than the output of the pumping stations, was stored by raising the weights in the accumulator towers by applying water pressure to the hydraulic rams. When demand from the system exceeded the power available from the pumping stations the shortfall was met by allowing the accumulator weights to fall, thus depressing the hydraulic rams which increased the pressure within the system. Control equipment within the towers automatically reduced the speed of the pumps as the accumulators neared their maximum capacity. At the consumer's end of the system, power was transmitted linearly by means of hydraulic pistons while rotary motion was obtained by means of turbines or Pelton wheels.

The distribution system consisted of a network of wrought and cast-iron pipes varying between two inches and ten inches in diameter and laid either directly in the ground beneath roads and pavements or, in the case of the larger diameter mains, carried in purpose-built subterranean tunnels. The larger tunnels had the advantages that connections to new customers could be more readily facilitated, capacity could be easily increased by laying additional pipelines, and there was the possibility of leasing space to other service providers.

By the 1970s demand had dropped away due to the shift from hydraulic to electric power for most industrial applications, and in 1977 pumping ceased and the system was closed down. But what remained was a valuable asset, for the company owned a network of underground ducts that served most of London north of the Thames (and parts to the south), and it also, as a Statutory Authority, had the legal right to dig up the public highway to install and maintain its pipes. The potential value of these assets and powers was immense at the time that digital systems were revolutionising communications in the City, for they provided ready-made ducts for fibre-optic cables at minimal cost, with the right to dig up the roadway to lay new ducts with little interference from the local authorities.

Below: The hydraulic power mains pass beneath the Thames through the Tower Subway, acquired by the London Hydraulic Power Company in 1893. The northern access is via this kiosk (which is not original) on Tower Hill.

Above: Hydraulic power mains in a very large service tunnel that runs beneath Rosebery
Avenue. Access to the tunnel is gained from beneath a bridge in Warner Street.

Chapter 19

ABBEY MILLS PUMPING STATION

Above: A pre-war view of Abbey Mills pumping station taken prior to the demolition of the twin chimneys.

Until the middle of the nineteenth century London's sewage flowed untreated into the Thames. It came from street gutters, overflows from cesspits, and from the City's primitive sewers that were beginning to proliferate following the gradual introduction of flush toilets from the 1840s. The effect was that the Thames became one vast and unwholesome open sewer, creating serious consequences due to the peculiar tidal nature of the river. Daily, the accumulated filth and ordure would move slowly downstream with the river's flow, only to be pushed back up to the heart of the City as the tide rose in the estuary.

From the 1830s cholera epidemics were rife in London but the link between the disease and the quality of the City's drinking water was only slowly being appreciated and there was a general reluctance to accept the concept of such a causal relationship. Even John Snow's compelling statistical evidence of a direct link between an outbreak of cholera in Soho in 1854 and an identifiable, contaminated drinking water standpipe met with much resistance. What concerned the authorities more was the stench, or miasma, produced by the sewage-laden river, and in 1848 the Metropolitan Commission of Sewers was

Above: The newly restored lantern that stands above the crossing point of the four bays of the cruciform engine house.

Above: The truncated base of the eastern chimney stack, seen from the roof of the pumping station.

set up to look into the problem. Little was done, however, until the unusually hot summer of 1858, the year of the Great Stink when the heat caused the stench from the Thames to become unbearable. In Westminster the situation was so bad that curtains soaked in chloride of lime were hung across the windows of the Houses of Parliament to ward off the odours and proposals were made to move both Houses up-river to Hampton Court. The following year the Metropolitan Board of Works, successor to the earlier and ineffective Commission of Sewers initiated a thorough inquiry into the problem.

The outcome of the inquiry was the acceptance of Joseph Bazalgette's scheme for a series of six huge interceptor sewers running parallel to the Thames, three north of the river and three south, to carry the City's sewage eastwards along the estuary to a point where it would not be washed back in as the tide turned. The new sewers, as their names suggest, intercepted the old north-south oriented sewers that disgorged directly into the Thames. The lowest of the northern interceptors runs beneath the Thames Embankment which was constructed between 1862 and 1870. At their eastern extremities the interceptor sewers feed into the northern and southern outfall sewers which, when first constructed, emptied into huge lagoons at Becton and Crossness where the sewage was stored untreated until the tide was right to carry it out to sea. Later, treatment works were constructed to process the sewage before it was released.

Most of the system worked by gravity but, at Chelsea and Deptford, pumping stations were built to raise the sewage to the height necessary to produce a sufficient flow. Two further pumping stations were built at Crossness and Abbey Mills to raise the combined contents of the interceptor sewers to the level of the outflow sewers.

The Abbey Mills pumping station, designed by Joseph Bazalgette, Edmund Cooper and the architect Charles Driver, was completed in 1868 and housed eight beam engines arranged in groups of two in each bay of an impressively ornate cruciform engine-house. An underground boiler-house enclosing sixteen coal-fired Lancashire boilers was built to the northeast of the main engine-house. A 1,000-ton-capacity underground coal store was built nearby, consisting of sixteen vaulted stone bays each 100 feet long and four smaller bays 85 feet long. A system of rails and trolleys connected the boiler-house to the coal store. On the surface four lines of rails brought coal from a wharf on the Thames to the pumping station where it was discharged through hatches into the underground coal yard below.

The steam pumping plant was taken out of use in 1933 and replaced by electric pumps. During the Second World War the two prominent boiler-house chimneys were demolished as it was thought that they provided an obvious navigational landmark for enemy bombers. It was also feared that had they been damaged by enemy action there was a risk that they might fall into the engine-house and damage the electric pumps, which would have had very serious consequences for the population of London. In recent years a new pumping station has been built on the site but the original electric pumps in the 1868 engine-house have been retained as standby units. In 2012 all except two bays of the underground coal yard were filled with foam concrete after concern was raised regarding their stability.

Right: Sectional plan of Abbey Mills pumping station showing the underground boiler-houses and coal vaults to the north of the engine-house.

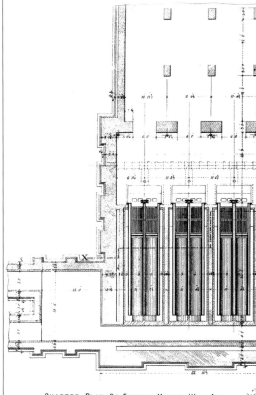

QUARTER PLAN OF ENGINE HOUSE WALL AND FLY WHEEL & CRANK RACES ON LINE g. h. ON SECTIONS (ENGINES e.f. ON SECTIONS)

SECTIONAL PLAN OF

ENGINE AND BOILER HOUSES

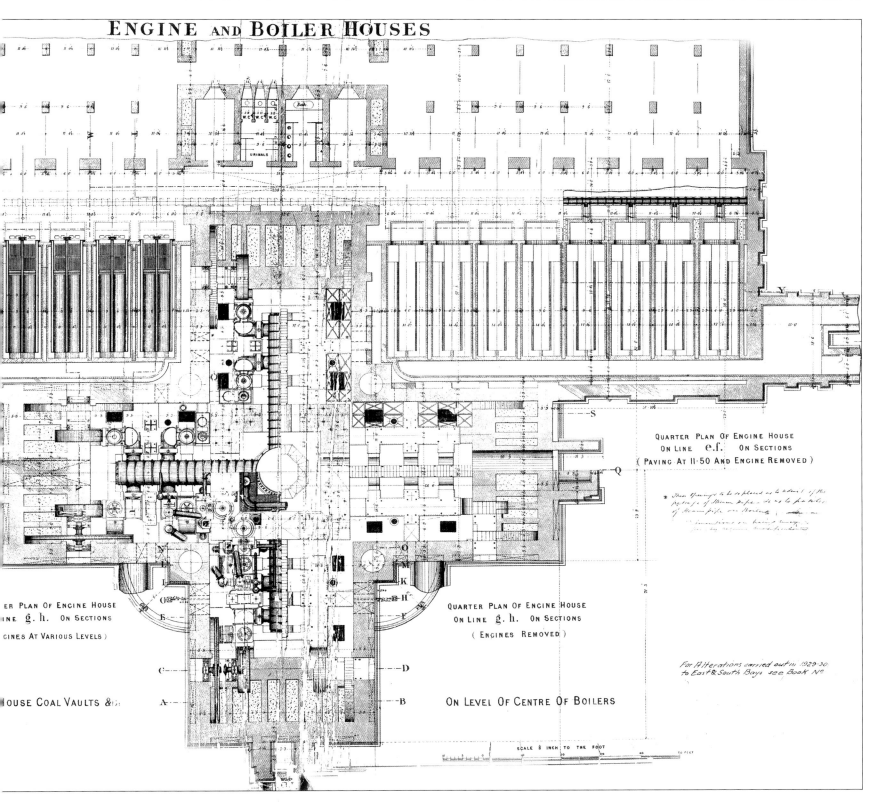

QUARTER PLAN OF ENGINE HOUSE
ON LINE e.f. ON SECTIONS
(PAVING AT 11·50 AND ENGINE REMOVED)

QUARTER PLAN OF ENGINE HOUSE
ON LINE g.h. ON SECTIONS
(ENGINES REMOVED)

ER PLAN OF ENGINE HOUSE
INE g.h. ON SECTIONS
(CINES AT VARIOUS LEVELS)

OUSE COAL VAULTS &

ON LEVEL OF CENTRE OF BOILERS

For Alterations carried out in 1929-30
to East & South Bays see Book No

SCALE ⅛ INCH TO THE FOOT

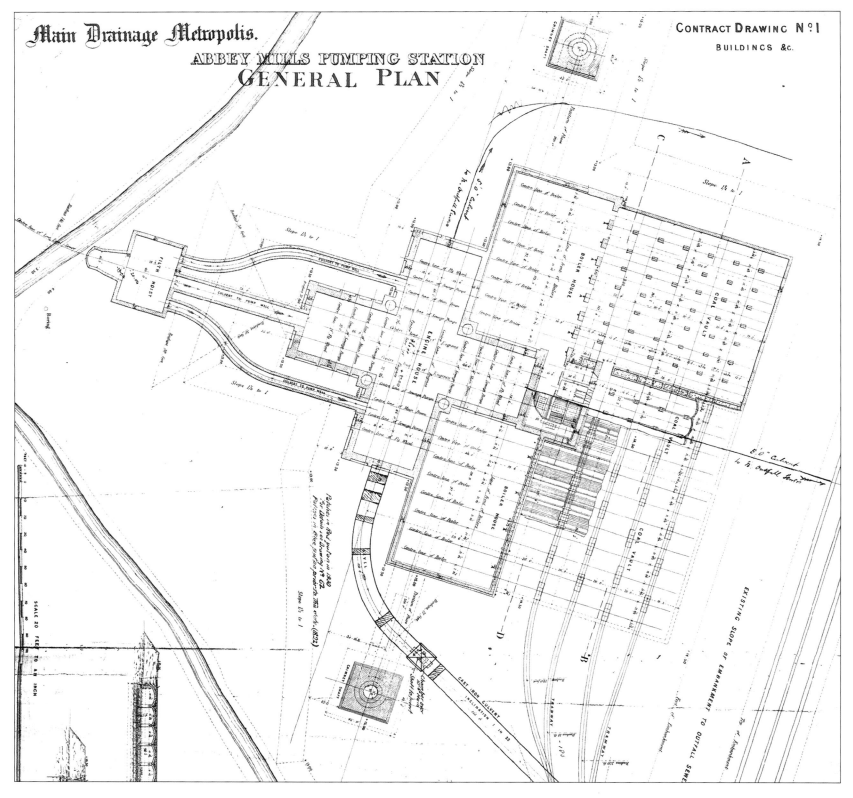

Opposite: General arrangement plan of the pumping station and full extent of the coal vaults. Sewage enters the site via the low-level sewer and filth hoist to the left of the plan and leaves via the cast-iron culvert at centre bottom to join the main outfall sewer.

Above: A surviving section of the underground coal vaults, before infilling in 2012. Bays in the background have already been backfilled with debris.

Chapter 20

THAMES BARRIER SERVICE TUNNELS

Above: Thames Barrier pier No.9, seen from the south abutment. The section of tunnel beneath this pier can be seen on page 238.

The Thames Barrier extends for 520 metres across the river from Silvertown on the north bank to New Charlton in Greenwich on the south bank. The concept of the barrier, the role of which is to prevent the flooding of central London in event of an exceptionally high tide or storm surge in the North Sea, was first given serious consideration after the floods of 1953 which killed 307 people. There was growing concern, too, that sea levels, which had been rising at a rate of approximately 20cm each century, together with the slow but perceptible tilt downwards of the eastern land mass of the British Isles would only accentuate the risk in the longer

term. The requirements of commercial shipping on the Thames, however, prevented practical progress until the early 1970s by which time much of London's shipping had become containerised and concentrated upon the rapidly expanding docks at Tilbury. With only smaller vessels passing up the Thames, the barrier became a practical possibility. Construction work on the mammoth undertaking began in 1974 and was completed in 1984. As well as the principal barrier that spans the width of the river, there are also subsidiary barriers at

Barking, King George V Lock, Dartford, Tilbury Docks and Canvey Island that also have to be closed, along with the main barrier, in order to afford effective protection further up-river.

The main structure consists of nine piers and two shore abutments creating six navigable spans and four non-navigable. Of the former, four are 61 metres wide and two are 30 metres wide. The barrier gates themselves consist of circular segments that rotate about pivots mounted on the intermediate and shore piers. When not raised they lie in segmental concrete lintels on the bed of the river. The four largest gates each weigh 3,700 tons and are over 20 metres high.

Two twin continuous personnel and service tunnels run through the full length of barrier, through the lintels both upstream and downstream of the gates. These allow pedestrian access to all the intermediate piers without obstructing navigation in any way, while also providing a route for all the power and communication cables and other necessary service pipes and conduits that need to be accessible for maintenance. Lifts and pedestrian stairways rise from the access tunnels into each of the piers.

Below: The upstream service tunnel from the south shore abutment looking north beneath the river.

Above: The upstream tunnel beneath pier No.9, looking towards the south abutment. The racking on the left-hand side carries power, control and communications cabling. The large black pipes on the right are hydrant mains and a sprinkler main for fire protection. A fire alarm and smoke sensor can be seen to the top left of this view.

Chapter 21

CEMETERY CATACOMBS

Above: The northwest quadrant of the colonnade at Brompton Cemetery.

For almost a thousand years Christians disposed of their dead by burial in consecrated ground attached to a church or, for those of particular consequence, beneath the church itself. Certainly in Western Europe exceptions to this rule are scarce and relatively recent, the mausoleum built at Castle Howard by Hawksmoor for the Third Earl of Carlisle (died 1738) being the earliest recorded example in modern times. The rapid increase in Britain's population (from five million in 1701 to eight million in 1801, sixteen million in 1851 and thirty million in 1901), together with the drift of the labouring classes from country to town, saw huge concentrations of population in the larger cities, most particularly in London, making traditional churchyard burials impossible due simply to the scale of death. By the 1830s overcrowded city churchyards and vaults were identified as possible causes of cholera, and in 1832 the government took the first steps towards alleviating the problem.

In 1832, Parliament passed an Act allowing private, joint-stock companies to establish seven large, commercial cemeteries outside the boundaries of the City of London. In the order in which the first interments were made, they are:

Kensal Green, or the General Cemetery of All Souls, Kensal Green, opened by the General Cemetery Company in 1832.

West Norwood Cemetery, opened by the South Metropolitan Cemetery Company in 1837.

Highgate Cemetery, opened by the London Cemetery Company in 1839 on seventeen acres of land purchased from the Ashurst estate.

Abney Park Cemetery in Stoke Newington, opened in 1840. Abney Park was a non-denominational cemetery with its origins closely linked to the Congregationalist movement and the London

Missionary Society, but taken over by the strictly commercial General Cemetery Company in the 1880s.

Nunhead Cemetery, a fifty-two-acre site opened by the London Necropolis Company in 1840.

Brompton Cemetery, originally known as the West London and Westminster Cemetery, opened in 1840. Brompton proved financially unsuccessful and was bought out by the government, to the relief of its shareholders, under the terms of 1850 Metropolitan Interments Act.

Tower Hamlets Cemetery, opened by the City of London and Tower Hamlets Cemetery Company in 1841. After the Second World War the cemetery fell into disrepair and interments ceased in 1966, shortly after which it was purchased by the Greater London Council for £100,000. The site was transferred to Tower Hamlets Borough Council in 1986 and since then the chapels and many of the gravestones have been cleared to provide a public open space.

The Catacombs

Three of the London cemeteries, South Norwood, Kensal Green and Brompton, provided underground vaults or catacombs as alternatives to conventional earthen graves, in which coffins, their wooden carcasses enclosing sealed lead liners, were stacked one upon the other, or upon stones shelves or iron rails, depending upon the fancy of the families who purchased space there. It was quite possible to purchase accommodation for a single coffin, or for a whole vault dedicated to one's family which might be left open, or secured by ornate iron gates or sealed by a stone wall depending, once again, upon the whim of the family concerned. A family vault could be a very grand affair, but when first envisaged by the cemetery companies they were seen as a less expensive option to conventional burial and a more efficient use of the available space. At West Norwood, separate catacombs were provided for Anglicans and Dissenters, but the latter was not popular and many of the 4,000 or so vaults remained unoccupied. At Brompton, too, the catacombs were under-subscribed and the West London & Westminster Cemetery Company, cutting its anticipated losses, abandoned further construction after only 500 of the proposed 4,000 spaces had been completed.

Right: A well-populated section of the catacomb at Brompton Cemetery. The curve of the vault, following the circular sweep of the colonnade above, is evident in this photograph.

Brompton Cemetery

Brompton Cemetery, now managed by the Royal Parks Agency following its acquisition by the government under the short-lived 1850 Metropolitan Interments Act, was designed by Benjamin Baud and has at its centre a domed chapel reached by long, curving colonnades and flanked by catacombs. Beatrix Potter, author of the famous Peter Rabbit children's stories, lived nearby at a house called

The Boltons and the names of many of her animal characters are taken from headstones in the cemetery. It has been suggested, too, that Mr McGregor's fictional walled garden is based upon the design of the chapel colonnades. Burials ceased at Brompton in 1952 but resumed in 1996 with plots for burials and a Garden of Remembrance for the deposit of cremated remains.

Below: Demand for accommodation in the catacomb at Brompton Cemetery was disappointing and many of the vaults and shelves remain unoccupied.

Kensal Green Cemetery

Right: Three catacombs were constructed at Kensal Green. One lies beneath the North Terrace Colonnade, which is now sealed, and another beneath the Dissenters' Chapel at the east end of the cemetery, which was severely damaged by bombing during the Second World War and is no longer open. The third, situated in the centre of the cemetery beneath the Episcopal Chapel of 1837, is still accessible and has space remaining for further interments.

The architecture at Kensal Green is somewhat more sophisticated than at Brompton. Here the underground aisles which divide the catacomb have complex cross-vaulted ceilings, and where the arches meet the bosses are open, allowing a small amount of light to percolate through from above. The catacomb has space for 4,000 deposits and currently contains approximately 2,500 coffins. The whole cemetery is the final resting place of some 250,000 bodies in 65,000 graves.

Overleaf: The Kensal Green hydraulic coffin lift. Shortly after the cemetery was opened a screw-jack coffin lift was installed in the catacomb beneath the Episcopal Chapel to enable coffins to be lowered gracefully through the floor of the chapel after the service of commendation and committal. This device proved to be both unreliable and intrusively noisy and, in 1844, it was replaced by a Bramah & Robinson hydraulic lift similar, though not identical, to the machine recently installed at West Norwood Cemetery. At Kensal Green the mechanism moved the entire catafalque, rather than just the platform upon which the coffin rests, and thus required a more powerful, two-handled twin-cylinder hydraulic pump. The long-derelict coffin lift was restored and brought back into working order by the Friends of Kensal Green Cemetery in 1997. The hand-wheel and vertical rod seen in this photograph control a bypass valve which, when opened, allows the catafalque to descend slowly and silently into the catacomb below.

West Norwood Cemetery

Two interment chapels were built at West Norwood, the Anglican on the high ground and the Dissenters' chapel lower down the hillside. Underground catacombs, brick-walled with brick-arched ceilings, were constructed beneath each chapel. By 1900 both the burial ground and the Anglican catacomb were largely filled and, to cope with the continued flow of corpses, a crematorium and columbarium (a resting place for the cremated ashes of the deceased) were built beside the Dissenters' chapel in 1915. In 1955 the Dissenters' chapel and the early crematorium were demolished and a modern crematorium built on the site, the furnaces being housed in the vaults of the Dissenters' catacomb. The fate of the displaced coffins is unrecorded. A few years later, in 1960, the Anglican chapel was demolished and a rose garden laid out on its former site. The catacombs below, containing some 2,500 coffins and an early hydraulic coffin-lift, survive intact.

Right: This enamel sign identifies the South Metropolitan Cemetery Company as the original proprietors of West Norwood Cemetery. By the middle of the twentieth-century the company was running short of land in which to make further burials and, deprived of its principal source of income, found itself in financial difficulties. Without funds for its maintenance the cemetery fell into disrepair and was compulsorily purchased by Lambeth Council in 1965.

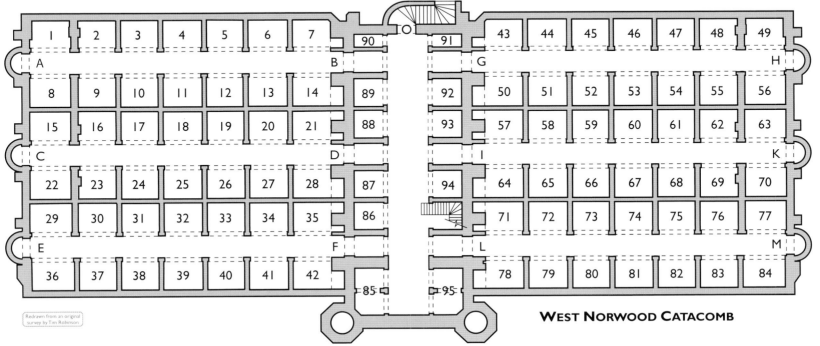

WEST NORWOOD CATACOMB

Redrawn from an original survey by Tim Robinson

Opposite: The decaying remains of the Bramah hydraulic lift at West Norwood Cemetery, installed in 1839. Unlike the modified lift at Kensal Green, the hydraulic mechanism at West Norwood raised and lowered only the horizontal platform of the catafalque. Following the demolition of the Anglican chapel and its replacement by a rose garden, the opening in the ceiling through which coffins were lowered was sealed, as was a nearby flight of stairs which led up into the chapel.

When the first Tousoil Fradet & Cie gas cremator was installed in the little-used catacomb beneath the Dissenters' chapel in 1915, a similar Bramah hydraulic lift was used to lower the coffins. From there a narrow gauge railway system, complete with marshalling yard and storage sidings, transported coffins to the cremator. All this was swept aside after the First World War when more modern cremators were installed.

Right: Coffins closely stacked in a bay at West Norwood. Many of these appear to be children's coffins. The density, and consequent economy, with which it is possible to accommodate the dead in catacombs, as opposed to conventional graveyard burials, is evident in this photograph.

Overleaf: More coffins stacked in a side-aisle at West Norwood. In the background light percolates into the catacomb from a grated opening located just beyond the edge of the rose garden above.

Chapter 22

CHALK & SAND MINES

Dartford Chalk Mine

From 1886 until shortly before the First World War C. N. Kidd operated a brickyard off Shepherd's Lane in Dartford and also had a brewery business nearby. To supply raw material for the brickworks a large, open clay pit was established on the north side of Shepherd's Lane and later this was linked via a tunnel to a smaller pit on the south side. Clay was dug to a depth of about thirteen or fourteen feet. Some thirty feet beneath the clay there lies a deep stratum of chalk, and in order to mine this material Kidd sunk a vertical shaft beneath the eastern end of the clay pit situated south of the lane. A crushing plant was established near the shaft and a series of washing and settling ponds was built some distance away. This was a precaution against the risk of one of the ponds bursting and flooding the underground workings, as had happened with disastrous effect at Cemetery Mine near Plumstead a short while earlier.

A well had been sunk close to the mine shaft and in 1920, some years after the underground workings had fallen into disuse, and probably after the mine shaft had been blocked, a surface drain was

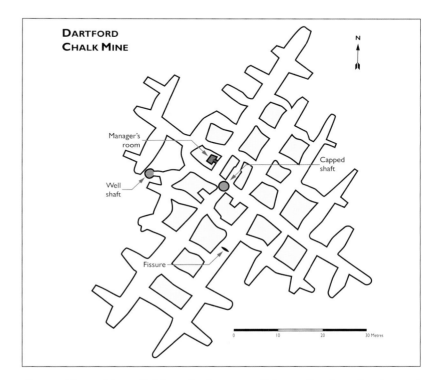

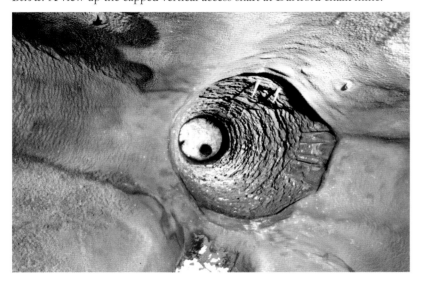

Below: A view up the capped vertical access shaft at Dartford chalk mine.

directed into this well. Near the bottom of the well a short horizontal tunnel was bored into the mine to redirect the flow of water into the old workings which then acted as a soakaway. After the mine ceased production the entrance was completely lost beneath waste material, including large quantities of broken glass, dumped in the former brickyard by Kidd's brewery, but the well remained accessible. In 1980 members of the Kent Underground Research Group gained access to the mine via the well shaft and completed a survey of the workings which, they deduced from the evidence of tide-marks on the wall, had at times been flooded to a depth of five feet. Houses were built on the site in 1988 and parts of the mine were rock-bolted and concreted at that time to ensure the stability of their foundations. A secure manhole and ladder were fitted to the well to allow for periodic inspection.

Above: A typical passageway in Dartford chalk mine showing the characteristic elongated arch formation, which allowed the maximum amount of mineral to be extracted without the need for expensive artificial roof supports. The reclining figure in the background indicates the scale of the workings. Extraction started at the top level of the chalk stratum in the mine and progressed downwards.

Pinner Chalk Mine

Chalk, mainly for agricultural use, was extracted from underground workings in Pinner for a period of approximately forty years, from the 1830s until the 1870s. Competition from cheaper and better materials brought in from further afield by rail brought about the demise of local production. The chalk, which lies approximately fifty to sixty feet below the surface, was extracted via vertical shafts. Three such shafts are known to have been sunk, the first in 1830 on land to the north of the Stanmore to Uxbridge road to the rear of Dingles Court. It would appear that the heading from this working ran into an unstable area of running red sand and, in 1840, a new shaft was sunk some distance to the northeast of the original workings. Eventually this too encountered a further area of unstable ground to the north, while a westward expansion of the mine ran into the earlier 1830s workings. A third shaft, sunk in 1850, continued to produce chalk until the mid-1870s when demand collapsed.

The 1830 shaft has now been lost as a result of later opencast extraction in the area, and the shaft of 1840 has been sealed, but controlled access to the 1850 shaft is still possible via the manhole-cover fitted by Harrow Borough Council during the early 1960s. The entrance lies in woods behind Dingles Court to the east of the Montesole playing fields on Pinner Green.

Above: The 'bench' at the end of this heading indicates that chalk was extracted in layers, working down from ceiling level.
Below left: A view looking up the vertical access shaft. The bottom section of the shaft appears to be lined with well bricks.
Below right: Another 'bench' is visible at the far end of this passageway.

Above: In a manner similar to that employed at the Dartford chalk mine, here the mineral has been extracted to the fullest extent possible without resort to artificial roof supports. The sound ceiling stratum has allowed the tunnels here to be cut to a truncated arch section. Note the horizontal bands of tabular flint and rows of flint nodules. This material was not left in the quarry but was probably taken out for road-making and building.

Above: The entrance portal to the inclined access tunnel into Diamond Terrace sand mine.

Diamond Terrace Sand Mine

Local rumour had long suggested that there was a lost underground sand mine in the Hyde Vale area of Greenwich. To support the rumours, there were vague documentary pointers to it having been near Nightingale Lane, a road now long-gone but which is known to have followed the course of the present Westgrove Lane. Initial investigations by local historians proved fruitless and it was assumed that the entrance had been built over when the area was developed for housing. Then, in 1985, an entrance was found, open and accessible, in the garden of a house in Diamond Terrace one hundred yards or so to the north of Westgrove Lane.

An arched entrance gave access to a flight of steps and a long, brick-lined inclined passage. The mine consists of three main galleries and two cross-passages. The explorers found some roof-falls and an area that had been reinforced with concrete and corrugated iron, which it is assumed was put in place during the Second World War when the mine was used as an air-raid shelter.

The use to which the material dug from the mine was put is debateable. Diamond Terrace mine lies in a bed of Thanet sand which occurs extensively between the Isle of Thanet and east Surrey. Extensive use is made of the coarser grades as common builders' sand. Most of the Greenwich glassworks operating from the seventeenth to the nineteenth century used a fine, hard white sand from the Lower Greensand found east of Maidstone for their best white glass, but Upper Thanet sand was used to make low-grade green glass for bottles. Sand from Diamond Terrace may have been used in glass production, but it lies in a stratum of Lower Thanet sand which was more commonly used as a moulding sand for iron founding, or in brickyards to prevent bricks sticking in the moulds. The abundance of Thanet sand suitable for mould-making was one of the principal reasons for the War Office concentrating its cannon-making capacity at Woolwich.

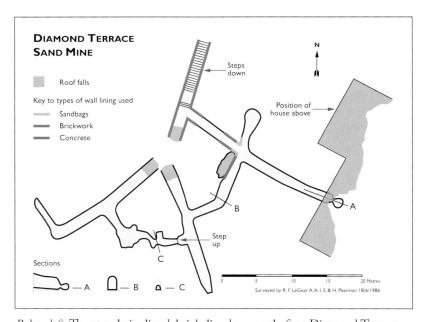

Below left: The steeply inclined, brick-lined access shaft at Diamond Terrace.

Below right: Sandbags and diagonal struts used to reinforce the section of the sand mine used as a domestic air-raid shelter during the Second World War.

Above: A view along the passageway branching eastwards from the bottom of the inclined shaft, looking through the brick-lined section towards the sandbag-reinforced area. The uneven nature of the tunnels is evident in this picture.

Chapter 23

SURREY STONE QUARRIES

London and its environs are not immediately recognised as major stone-producing areas and there is little evidence that the City has emerged organically from its natural environment in the way that, for example, Bath and Paris grew out of the underlying limestone. Indeed, most of the major buildings in London, particularly those built after the Great Fire (and most have been built after the Great Fire), are of brick or, in the case of the most prestigious buildings, of Portland stone. There are, of course, a few earlier survivors and these, for the most part, are constructed from what must be regarded as the nearest that London has to an indigenous building material, the Upper Greensand of east Surrey, often, and not always accurately, described as Reigate stone.

The majority of the quarries are located in an area underneath the foot of the chalk escarpment of the North Downs stretching from the parish of Brockham in the west to Godstone in the east, with concentrations in the vicinities of Merstham and of Reigate Hill and the Godstone Gap, which in earlier centuries were the principal transport routes northwards into London. The quarries, which lie approximately twenty to one hundred feet below ground level, were worked northwards into the hillside on a slight down-dip. Headings in the larger quarries extend for approximately 1,000 feet into the hill where, because of the down-dip, they encounter the water table and become unworkable.

The Upper Greensand is a soft, fine-grained stone, a pleasant greenish-cream in colour, reminiscent of the oolitic limestones of the Bath and Portland areas. It is an easily worked stone but, if badly selected, does not weather well, and for this reason it fell out of favour towards the end of the eighteenth century as the growth of the canal system made the transportation of the far superior Bath, Portland and Oxfordshire stones cheaper. Despite its shortcomings, Upper Greensand has been used as a building stone for more than a thousand years. It is found in a number of surviving Saxon churches and was much used for ecclesiastical buildings from the twelfth century onwards. During the previous century, following the Norman Conquest, Caen stone had been favoured by the immigrant

masons who were more familiar with their native material. During the fourteenth century Upper Greensand was used for the rebuilding of Windsor Castle, Westminster Abbey and Canterbury Cathedral. Through the fifteenth and sixteenth centuries it fell gradually out of favour although it still found use as a building stone, to a lesser degree, into the eighteenth century. In 1713 Sir Christopher Wren, although writing disparagingly about the weathering properties of Reigate stone, still ordered considerable quantities of it for internal construction work in St. Paul's cathedral. The exterior of the cathedral exposed to the elements is, however, clad in Portland stone.

Towards the middle of the eighteenth century the ailing Upper Greensand quarries underwent something of a resurgence as new uses were found for the stone which, it was discovered, had particular characteristics which had not to any great extent been previously capitalised upon. It was realised that the stone was to a large extent impervious to the effects of heat and fire, which made it an ideal refractory material for domestic fireplaces, chimneys and industrial furnaces. Surrey Firestone, as it became known, found a ready market in the annealing kilns of the many small glassworks in southeast England, but by the 1850s it was being exported throughout the whole of Britain, a trade facilitated by the rapidly expanding railway network. A peculiar combination of late-Victorian and Edwardian architecture and domestic culture created yet another improbable market for Upper Greensand that rose to prominence just as the demand for firestone began to decline. Certain grades of Upper Greensand were marketed as 'hearthstone' and used to whiten the doorsteps, windowsills and hearths of the middle-class homes of England. At first, hearthstone was sold in rough, hand-sized lumps and these, rubbed by housewives and servants onto domestic hearths and windowsills imparted a smooth and clean white surface that was the envy of the neighbours. Later, in the early twentieth century, the stone was ground, mixed with a cement filler and pressed into regular shaped blocks, often impressed with a trade-name, rather than sold as rough block. This trade was short-lived and went into decline after the First World War when domestic servants were less readily available and household priorities changed. Efforts were made, right up until the Second World War and beyond, to maintain the trade by marketing hearthstone as a finely-ground powder that could be sprinkled and then buffed to a smooth finish, rather than laboriously rubbed in block form onto the surfaces to be treated. The last working Surrey hearthstone mine, at Colley Hill, Reigate, closed around 1961.

Shortly before the First World War and into the inter-war years many of the worked-out quarries, notably those in the Godstone area, found new uses as underground mushroom farms. During this period the production of mushrooms as a delicacy developed dramatically, driven by the discerning demands of the new luxury liners then being built and from London's sumptuous new hotels. Environmental conditions within the quarries were near perfect for the cultivation of mushrooms, and little work was required other than clearing and levelling the floors and erecting doors at certain points within the workings to control the flow of air. A number of vertical ventilation shafts were sunk at the innermost ends of some of the quarries to further aid the circulation of air and these were sometimes fitted with electric fans. Cultivation in some quarries continued up until the Second World War, but their lifetimes were limited. Mushrooms are notoriously vulnerable to various fungal and other infections that, once present, are terminal and ineradicable. It is inevitable that eventually the crop will fail through disease and the quarry will have to be abandoned.

A few of the quarries in the Godstone area were called upon to perform one last service during the Second World War as secure repositories for stocks evacuated from vulnerable locations in London by several of the City's prominent wine and spirit merchants, as a private bonded warehouse and as a place of safety for exhibits from the Natural History Museum. Since the war the quarries were very much forgotten about, with many of the more recent entrance adits blocked by tipping or obscured by later chalk quarrying activities. The locations of many earlier quarries, their existence hinted at only through obscure references in ancient leases, can only be guessed at, but it is assumed that they are numerous. The construction of the M23 and M25 motorways in the early 1970s renewed interest in the quarries, (for they caused the highway engineers considerable difficulties), and a great deal of research into their history has been on-going since that time.

A note on nomenclature: mineral workings that produced building materials are generally referred to as quarries, those that do not are referred to as mines. This is the convention adhered to in this chapter.

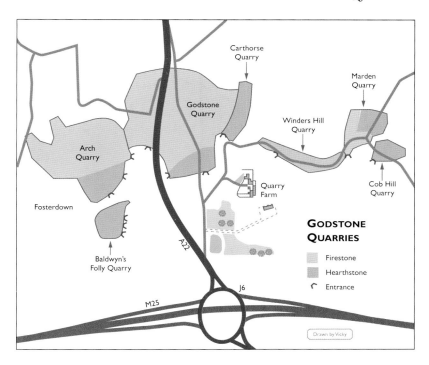

Arch Quarry

Below: Mushroom cultivation was begun in Arch Quarry around 1905 but was not a financially successful venture. This photograph shows some of the surviving beds of mushroom compost in the quarry.

Opposite: Timber roof props in Arch Quarry, probably erected during the time the workings were used for mushroom cultivation.

Above: A typical passageway in Arch Quarry. The floor has been cleared and levelled to allow easy access to the mushroom growing areas. The smoothly picked wall to the right suggests that this area of Arch was a building stone quarry

Carthorse Quarry

This page: During the Second World War Carthorse Quarry was occupied by a number of London wine and spirit merchants for the storage of stocks previously held in London warehouses which became vulnerable to bombing. Both the Natural History Museum and the Geological Museum, which was an independent institution until 1985, also made use of Carthorse Quarry as a secure, dispersed storage facility. Some sections of the workings were secured by makeshift iron gates, like that seen in the photograph to the right, at the entrance to Burgoynes storage area, while others were sealed by more substantial vault doors. Throughout the quarry conspicuous red direction signs point visitors towards the various repositories.

Godstone Hill Quarry

Right: The remaining horizontal adit entrance to Godstone Hill Quarry with access partially obscured by power-station ash that has been tipped in the surrounding open quarry workings.

Below left: Viewed from within the quarry, this brick arch reinforced the entrance to Jones's quarry which was contiguous with the western side of Godstone Hill Quarry, just to the east of the current A22 trunk road. The entrance was buried when the main road was widened and the surrounding area infilled with power-station ash.

Below right: This heavily timbered passageway, beyond the brick arch, shows evidence of substantial roof-falls. It is now the only link between Jones's Quarry and the rest of the workings at Godstone Hill.

Above: Surviving early cast-iron plateway rails in Godstone Hill Quarry. These are remarkably similar in design to the rails used on the Croydon Merstham & Godstone Iron Railway and it had been suggested that they were either laid underground in 1805, when the CM&GIR was built, or were acquired second-hand by the quarry owners when the assets of the railway company were auctioned following its closure in 1838. More recently some rails in the Surrey quarries have been discovered bearing the cast initials of the railway company, suggesting that they were indeed acquired following the demise of the CM&GIR.

Above: The plateway in this section of passage in Godstone Hill Quarry, in an area used for firestone and/or building stone extraction, has been removed leaving characteristic deep ruts in the floor. Note the piles of roughly-dressed stone used to create support pillars for suspect areas of roof. This was the earlier form of roof support employed by the Godstone quarrymen and resemble those in the stone quarries under parts of Paris.

Above right: Rectangular-section timber roof supports, like those seen here, are more typical of the areas adapted for mushroom cultivation in the years leading up to the First World War.

Right: The narrow gauge rails seen in this photograph are much later, perhaps twentieth century, and were probably used to carry skips of rough stone blocks for use as hearthstone.

Marden Quarry

Right: Open workings adjacent to the entrance to Marden Quarry have been infilled with waste material and access is now possible only via this buried concrete pipe.

Below: The wide expanse of roof seen in this area of Marden Quarry testifies to the soundness of the stone stratum found there. Note the characteristic support pillars constructed of cut stone blocks in the passageway to the right. The brick reinforcements seen to the left are relics of the quarry's wartime use as a bonded warehouse. Unlike nearby Carthorse Quarry, which was used by a number of merchants to store their stocks of tax-paid wines and spirits, Marden was occupied by a single company who used it under much more strictly controlled conditions as a bonded warehouse to house wines and spirits upon which no tax had yet been paid, prior to its release to the retail trade.

Right: Lengths of prefabricated Decauville track and an abandoned wheel-set in a heading in Marden Quarry. As in the other mines in the Godstone area, it is probable that the more modern rails were laid during the twentieth century during the revival of trade due to the short-lived boost in demand for hearthstone.

Below: The timber props seen in this heading in Marden Quarry are typical of those erected during the Second World War and are in an area that was probably incorporated into the bonded warehouse. The west side of the workings was clearly a building stone quarry with characteristic smoothly picked side walls.

Above: The entrance to the bonded warehouse in Marden Quarry, with a heavy-duty iron security door still in place. Note the lengths of old rails used to support the roof at this point, one of which appears to have been badly distorted as a result of the substantial roof-fall seen in the foreground.

Winders Hill Quarry

Right: The television presenter Michael Buerk stands outside the entrance to Winders Hill Quarry in 1994 during filming of a sequence for the documentary series *999*. The episode included a dramatised reconstruction of a mining accident in Cornwall but, as an economy measure, the production company wanted to film close to London, somewhere within easy reach of the southern sector of the M25 motorway. Following a consultation with the Wealden Cave and Mine Society they selected Winders Hill Quarry in Surrey as it offered the only suitably convincing adit entrance in the vicinity.

Below: A view of the main haulageway in Winders Hill Quarry close to the entrance. What appear to be lengths of displaced plateway are, in fact, modern steel channel girders used as temporary rails to assist in the removal of spoil as part of a project undertaken in 2006 on behalf of the Surrey Bat Group to create an open area for the benefit of the quarry's bat population.

Above: A view looking out from the entrance to Winders Hill quarry along the cutting leading into the adit. To the left of the passageway the temporary rails laid in 2006 for spoil removal have become embedded in the floor and have, at first glance, acquired a deceptively eighteenth century appearance.

Chaldon Bottom

Extensive medieval underground workings are known to exist in the Merstham area but much has been lost to infilling during the construction of the M23 motorway. Test bores during the building of the motorway revealed an extensive network of galleries between Quarry Dean, Ockley Wood and Bedlams Bank, and it is supposed that over time many of the older workings had run into one another. Those areas, and others further east towards Rockshaw, which were not infilled with pulverised fuel-ash grout in the 1970s are now only accessible via Bedlams Bank.

The extraction of stone for building purposes had ceased during the early eighteenth century and was never to resume in the quarries to the east of the area from Ockley Wood to Rockshaw. The workings in the Quarry Dean area to the west, however, were exploited from 1788, principally at first for firestone, by the Joliffe family upon their acquisition of Merstham Manor. The Joliffes were also the driving force behind the Croydon, Merstham and Godstone Iron Railway which, as an extension (by a distinct company) of the Surrey Iron Railway, had ambitions to forge a transport link between Portsmouth and the River Thames. The line, however, when completed in 1805, never reached further than Merstham, with its southern terminus near Quarry Dean. Although never fulfilling the aspirations of its proprietors, the line provided a useful outlet for Merstham firestone for a third of a century until its demise in 1837.

Right: Access to the underground workings at Chaldon Bottom is now gained via the manhole and vertical shaft seen in this photograph, at Bedlams Bank. From here underground passages link with the Ockley Wood workings to the west and the Chaldon Bottom and Rockshaw Quarries to the east.

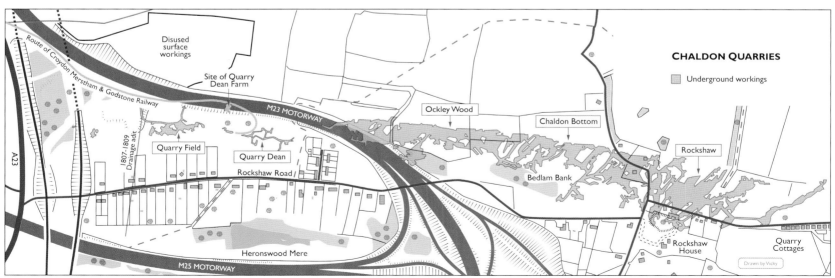

Left: The Surrey quarries were worked by the 'pillar and stall' method with the working faces, or 'stalls', between approximately eight and fourteen feet in width. The pillars left to support the roof were generally eight to ten feet square. Blocks of stone were split from the face using iron wedges to create fracture lines. In this photograph one of the wedges can be seen still in position in the horizontal break while the positions of three further wedges are evident along the vertical split. Quarrying ceased at Chaldon Bottom in the early eighteenth century, so the wedge seen here has lain embedded in the working face for some three hundred years.

Below: Several blocks of cut and roughly trimmed firestone in Chaldon Bottom stacked three centuries ago, ready for removal and sale.

Opposite: This view of a passageway in Chaldon Bottom vividly illustrates the instability of the roof in this area. Notice the joint line in the roof that extends down through the left-hand side of the pillar in the centre of the picture.

Right: A timber roof prop in Chaldon Bottom, almost completely rotted away. The original dimension can be gauged from the diameter of the hole at its base.

Below left: This ox skeleton was discovered during the exploration of an isolated section of Rockshaw Quarry that had been sealed off by a serious roof-fall in the distant past. It is probable that the ox was used as a draught animal for haulage in the quarry and, judging by the evidence of the hoof prints in the vicinity of the skeleton, it would seem it was trapped by the fall, tried frantically to escape, and subsequently died of starvation.

Below right: The presence of this horse skeleton on a main passageway some three hundred yards into the quarry is rather more puzzling. The entrance to the passage has only been blocked in relatively recent years and it is assumed that, while it was open, the horse had wandered in of its own accord and subsequently expired.

Above: A typical view in Rockshaw Quarry showing waste stone stacked neatly beside the haulageway.

Gatton Park

Gatton Park and Tower Wood quarries lie to the west of the A23 trunk road, south of the M25 motorway and a little to the north of the Royal Alexandra and Albert School. Both quarries, which were previously lost, were rediscovered in the 1970s when shafts collapsed into the workings. Quarries were known to have been worked at Gatton from at least as early as the seventeenth century, and one is recorded as active as late as 1858. Much of the stone can be seen in the estate buildings nearby.

Right: Excavations underway in 1986 to create a new secure entrance into Gatton Park Quarry.

Below left: The black pipe, formed from an oil drum, is the top of the new vertical shaft entrance to the quarry.

Below right: A general view of the underground workings at Gatton Park showing the large quantities of waste stone stacked beside the haulageway. In many of the quarries waste like this was later reprocessed to produce hearthstone powder or for pressing into block form.

Quarry Dean

Above left: The original entrance to Quarry Dean was a long vaulted passageway, but this was blocked by later landfill many years ago. However, when part of the arch collapsed the ensuing landslip created a new entrance through the roof of the tunnel. Quarry Dean was worked from about 1807 by the partnership of William Joliffe and Edward Banks, pioneering engineering contractors.

Above right: The blocked entrance tunnel showing the construction of the arched roof.

Left: In most of the Surrey quarries, waste stone was thrown back into the worked-out headings, but at Tower Wood, and in some parts of Quarry Dean, it was stacked down one side of the main passageways and contained behind carefully constructed dry stone walls.

Above: In this area of Quarry Dean it would appear that the waste has been dumped in a somewhat haphazard manner, or else the retaining walls have collapsed allowing the stone debris to spill across the floor.

Above: At its innermost end, Quarry Dean descends below the water table and is flooded as this photograph indicates. In 1807 a long drainage adit was excavated in an attempt to alleviate the problem but it interfered with the water supply to a nearby mill and resulted in a lawsuit in 1810. The adit collapsed around 1820 and the workings have been flooded ever since.

Chapter 24

EWELL HOUSE TUNNELS

Ewell House, a large, early eighteenth-century property that once stood to the west of Epsom Road in Ewell, on ground now occupied by Ewell House Grove, was demolished in 1962 to make way for a modern block of flats. The house and its surrounding land had gone into decline during the inter-war years and in the 1930s most of the grounds had been sold for housing development. Now, all that survives of the original property is a brick and timber summerhouse that once stood in the middle of the lawn, and fragments of the boundary wall.

Although the mansion is long gone, there still survives a fascinating network of underground passages that ran beneath the house and grounds, perhaps excavated when the house was built or possibly a century or so later. The history, purpose and full extent of the underground passages are obscure. Many of what may have been exit points from the tunnels around the perimeter of the grounds have been blocked, probably when the area was redeveloped in the 1930s, or possibly by roof-falls in later years. Much of the system, however, remains intact and in remarkably good order, but clues to its true function are few.

The tunnels are approximately six feet high and four feet wide and very roughly cruciform in plan, with each axis about 150 feet in length. Entrance from the main house was gained via a flight of steps at the far end of the eastern arm of the tunnels while a second entrance descended from the summerhouse to the crossing point of the two main axial passages. At this point there are two brick-vaulted chambers, one of which was once thought to be an ice-house, but its design makes it more likely to have been a cold-store or larder. The tunnels lie approximately fifteen feet below ground level and are excavated in a stratum of soft grey sand that would have been easily worked using simple hand tools. The eastern and southern arms appear to be the oldest and are brick-lined with an arched roof. The eastern arm, from the end of which a flight of steps led up to the cellars of the house, is particularly well constructed and features, near the bottom of the steps, a series of arched niches which bear resemblance to wine bins. The first thirty feet of this passage was at

Above: Ewell House, shortly before its demolition in 1962.

one time lit by gas. During the Second World War part of the system was used as an air-raid shelter and rudimentary electric lighting was installed.

It has been suggested that the earliest sections of tunnel were used as servants' and tradesmen's entrances, in order that the lower classes would be kept out of sight of the residents. There are national and local precedents for this; the historian Cloudesley S. Willis wrote of nearby Woodcote Grove (formerly Mount Diston), in Chalk Lane Epsom:

> 'In the cellar, which is below the basement, is a brick tunnel leading to a garden. Another tunnel runs from the road under the carriage drive, so that tradesmen calling at the kitchen door are not visible from the house.'

The other, more crudely excavated tunnels to the north and west are more difficult to explain and it has been suggested that they were dug as something of a subterranean folly, simply for the pleasure of amateur excavation.

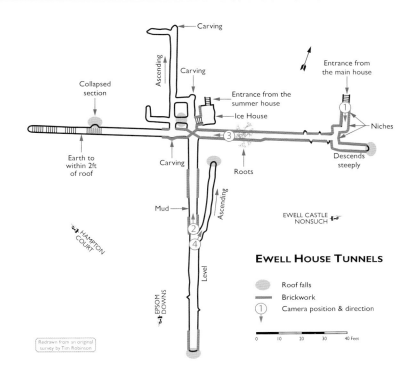

Above: Taken from position No.1 on the adjacent plan, at the bottom of a flight of steps leading from the basement of Ewell House, this photograph shows the short section of well-constructed, brick-lined passageway with a vaulted ceiling, lined on each side by what appear to be brick-arched wine bins. In the distance the passage turns sharply to the west and heads under the lawn towards the summerhouse.

Right: The main north-south passageway viewed from position No.2 on the plan, looking north towards the tunnel intersection below the summerhouse. Much of this passage is brick-lined with a barrel-vaulted ceiling and it appears to be of an earlier date than the more roughly excavated sections to the north and west. Behind the camera position the passage is blocked by a roof collapse, but it is possible that this tunnel once led to an alternative, inconspicuous entrance for tradesmen visiting the house.

Above: This photograph was taken from position No.3, looking across the intersection of the main axial passageways just south of the summerhouse. Beyond the crossing the tunnel is more roughly hewn and has partially collapsed in many places. Much of the graffiti is late nineteenth century.

Above: Looking north towards the main intersection from camera position No.4. The branch to the right climbs steeply and may once have gone to another entrance but is now blocked. Its purpose is unclear. Although the tunnels at this point are rough-hewn and unlined, the roof at the junction is supported by quite sophisticated brick cross-vaulting. The tunnel on the right collapsed in 2000 and has been infilled with concrete from the junction.

BIBLIOGRAPHY

Ackroyd, P, 2012, *London Under*, Vintage, ISBN: 9780099287377

Barton, N, 1996, *The Lost Rivers of London*, Phillimore & Co, ISBN:9780948667152

Beard, T and Emmerson A, 2007, *London's Secret Tubes*, Capital Transport Publishing, ISBN: 9781854143112

Burgess, P, 2008, *Surrey's Ancient Stone Mines*, Peter Burgess, ISBN: 9780955608117

Burgess, P, 2006, *East Surrey Underground*, Peter Burgess

Campbell, D, 1982, *War Plan UK: The Truth about Civil Defence in Britain*, Burnett Books, ISBN: 9780091506711

Catford, N, 2010, *Cold War Bunkers*, Folly Books, ISBN: 9780956440525

Clayton, A, 2010, *Subterranean City: Beneath the Streets of London*, Non Basic Stock Line, ISBN: 9781905286324

Cocroft, W D, Thomas, R J C, 2003, *Cold War: Building for Nuclear Confrontation 1946-89*, English Heritage, ISBN: 9781873592816

Connor, J E, 2000, *Abandoned Stations on London's Underground: A Photographic Record*, Connor & Butler, ISBN: 9780947699307

Dalton, M, 2011, *The Royal Observer Corps Underground Monitoring Posts*, Folly Books, ISBN: 9780956440556

Jackson, A A, Croome, D F, 1993, *Rails Through the Clay*, Capital Transport Publishing, ISBN: 9781854141514

Jones, C, 2003, *Subterranean Southwark*, Past Tense Publications

Laurie, P, 1979, *Beneath the City Streets*, Panther, ISBN: 9780586050552

Kent Underground Research Group, 1991, *Kent & East Sussex Underground*, Meresborough Books, ISBN: 9780948193583

Mansfield, I, 2012, *London's Lost Pneumatic Railways*, Kindle Edition, ASIN: B00ABXMXDI

Ozorak, P, 2012, *Underground Structures of the Cold War*, Pen & Sword, ISBN: 9781848844803

Pedroche, B, 2011, *Do Not Alight Here*, Capital Transport Publishing, ISBN: 9781854143525

Pennick, N, 1988, *Bunkers Under London*, Valknut Productions, ISBN: 9781871401004

Rule, F, 2012, *London's Labyrinth*, Ian Allan, ISBN: 9780711035447

Talling, P, 2011, *London's Lost Rivers*, Random House, ISBN: 9781849945976

Trench, R, Hillman, E, 1993, *London Under London: A Subterranean Guide*, John Murray, ISBN: 9780719552885

Wood, D, 1976, *Attack Warning Red: History of the Royal Observer Corps*, TBS The Book Service, ISBN: 9780356084114

Records of the Chelsea Speleological Society

The website of the underground research group *Subterranea Brittanica* (www.subbrit.org.uk) and the society's journal *Subterranea*, are particularly valuable resources for further study.